aquarium decorating and planning

Wilfried Weigel

translated by Gwynne Vevers

Distributed in the U.S.A. by T.F.H. Publications, Inc., 211 West Sylvania Avenue, P.O. Box 27, Neptune City, N.J. 07753; in England by T.F.H. (Gt. Britain) Ltd., 13 Nutley Lane, Reigate, Surrey; in Canada to the book store and library trade by Clarke, Irwin & Company, Clarwin House, 791 St. Clair Avenue West, Toronto 10, Ontario; in Canada to the pet trade by Rolf C. Hagen Ltd., 3225 Sartelon Street, Montreal 382, Quebec; in Southeast Asia by Y.W. Ong, 9 Lorong 36 Geylang, Singapore 14; in Australia and the south Pacific by Pet Imports Pty. Ltd., P.O. Box 149, Brookvale 2100, N.S.W., Australia. Published by T.F.H. Publications Inc. Ltd., The British Crown Colony of Hong Kong.

ISBN 0-87666-023-5

Contents

INTRODUCTION 4

1. AQUARIUM TECHNIQUE 5
   The biological background

2. SUGGESTED DESIGNS 13
   Like a picture on the wall . . . Made of cement
   . . . Some general considerations . . . How to set
   about it . . . An aquarium as partition wall . . .
   Tanks in a corner . . . Tall aquaria . . . A series
   of tanks . . . An aquarium cupboard . . . Small
   but good

3. MATERIALS 46
   Glass . . . Sealers . . . Cement . . . Rockwork . . .
   Glues . . . Plastics . . . Paints . . . Wood

4. THE DECORATION 56
   Do it yourself—but do it properly . . . Technical
   know-how . . . Kangaroos in a pine wood

5. SOME SUGGESTIONS FOR LANDSCAPE
   AQUARIA 78
   Waters in the lowlands of S.E. Asia . . . Mountain
   streams of S.E. Asia . . . Rain-forest waters of
   South America . . . The waters of an African rain-
   forest . . . Temperate marine aquaria . . . Tropical
   marine aquaria

INDEX 126

Introduction

The number of books on aquaria is very large. They tell us how to feed and breed fish, how to aerate, heat and clean the tank and how the water is affected chemically.

There is no doubt that these subjects are very important, but it is my opinion that these practical matters should not be allowed to obscure purely aesthetic values. An aquarium designed with care and taste can be a decorative feature and an eye-catcher in restaurants, offices and waiting rooms, as well as in living-rooms.

A properly decorated and furnished aquarium is not only beautiful but can at the same time be practical and biologically correct. So I do not intend to give abstract advice on aesthetic problems. This book is intended as a guide to setting up a decorative aquarium. The aquarist himself must look for the most suitable position in the room and decide on the size of the tank. He must decide on the materials and technical equipment to be used, but above all he must pay particular attention to the internal decoration of the tank. He must find rocks, sand and tree stumps and arrange them, he must plant the correct amount of aquatic vegetation and he must, of course, select suitable fish, in such number that each has sufficient living space.

An aquarium should be something that plants, fish and humans can enjoy.

1.

Aquarium Technique

I should like first of all to emphasize a few points in aquarium technique for the benefit of those readers who are not skilled aquarists.

It is possible that the reader will already have had thoughts about the ultimate position of his aquarium. He may even have exact ideas on its length, breadth and height. If, however, after reading this book, he has a feeling that another solution to the problem would have been more sensible, then he should start to plan again, because even in the aquarium world it pays to be up to date.

The decision on the size and proportions of the tank is closely tied to the question of materials. The larger the tank the greater is the pressure of water on the frame, cement and glass sides and of the whole installation on its foundation. In addition, there are certain items such as lighting, water circulation and so on which always become more of a problem as the size increases; it is indeed unfortunate that we require quite a battery of machinery and equipment to turn over a mere 10 gallons of water. It is astonishing the amount the aquarist has to learn about tanks, heaters, aerators and lighting before he can so much as dare to buy a couple of fish. In the beginning he must depend upon his petshop owner. Stay away from 5c and 10c stores!

An aquarium tank should be built in such a way that no corrosible metal parts can come into contact with water or condensation. During recent years a number of new materials have been used in aquarium construction. Thus, tanks can now be made in enamel-fired angle-iron or in anodized aluminium. There are tanks of PVC (polyvinyl chloride) and similar plastics. Tanks of asbestos cement are particularly good for sea water, but not as good as using sheets of plate-glass stuck together.

With the improvements in lighting equipment the window-sill has lost its position as the favorite place for a home aquarium. Nowadays a tank can be put in any position as long as it receives enough artificial light. An aquarium needs proper illumination, not only so that the contents can be seen, but above all to stimulate the growth of the plants. In some cases the spectral composition of the light is important, for certain wave-lengths affect growth in length, flowering and so on. The exact amounts and types of light required are still rather a matter of controversy, but quite a number of important facts have been discovered. See the book **"Light in the Aquarium"** for further details.

Most of the fish and plants used in aquaria come from tropical regions, and the tank water must be heated to and maintained at a certain temperature. In theory this problem has been solved by the use of electrical heaters and thermostats, although practice has shown that there is still room for improvement in the quality and precision of this equipment.

In a small enclosed tank, the chemical changes taking place in the water present a difficult problem, which is tied up with the biological relationships between the animals and plants. The water is being continuously fouled by animal excretion and it can only be kept clean for any length of time by installing an efficient filtration system. There are innumerable methods of filtering and purifying aquarium water. The most useful filter media are charcoal, quartz, nylon wool and more recently

6

certain foam plastics. Details of the working of a filter will be found in any good aquarium book. The plants will, of course, provide a certain amount of oxygen during the day, but in spite of this it is a good idea to supply oxygen by mechanical aeration, using a vibrating diaphragm pump with air diffusers or a circulating pump which squirts a jet of water onto the surface.

I know a number of aquarists who are horrified by the concept of aquarium technique. I always hear that an aquarium only functions properly if it is biologically balanced, and that one can do without the expense of technical equipment. I find this a somewhat unsound line of thought. If an aquarium is well equipped technically the aquarist will have at his disposal a number of alternative methods for dealing with every eventuality. When something goes wrong biologically there will be a greater chance that one or more of the technical aids will put it right. It is, of course, important that all technical equipment should be completely reliable. The value of good technique is surely reflected in the ever increasing number of beautiful and efficient aquarium tanks.

The biological background

For years, observation of biological processes, such as feeding, breeding, growth and regeneration and the rather useless flirtation with the invisible processes have been the most important aspects of aquarium work. It is only more recently, however, that these processes have been shown seriously to influence the chemistry of the water. Today we know a lot about oxygen and nitrogen economy, salinity and pH changes, protein breakdown and so on. These factors determine what happens in an aquarium and the more the aquarist understands them the easier will it be for him to solve his aquarium problems.

Most freshwater fish require a relatively soft, slightly acid water, and there is no difficulty in producing this. But it is usually more difficult to keep these conditions constant in the aquarium. It is all too easy for the water to become alkaline and for the concentration of nitrate to increase as a result of protein breakdown. The plants, on the other hand, need such inorganic salts. This and the fact that they give off oxygen during the day makes them the aquarist's friends. So we can see that theoretically the tank as a whole should be capable of regulating itself. This may happen in nature, but unfortunately it does not do so in an aquarium tank.

In the course of time fish can acclimatize themselves very well to a gradual increase in the nitrate content of the water and within certain limits will remain quite healthy. But new fish placed in such old, nitrate-rich water will probably be injured. In normal circumstances every healthy fish has sufficient powers of resistance to deal with disease vectors. But aquarium fish are often weakened by unsuitable environmental conditions and are then no longer able to master an infection. It is therefore not always the fault of the dealer if aquarium fish become ill and even die as soon as you put them into your aquarium.

Almost all water impurities can be analysed chemically and removed, at least partially, by mechanical, chemical or electrochemical methods. For some aquarists it may be quite amusing to have a small chemical laboratory alongside the aquarium, but for most this is rather too complicated. There are, of course, simple practical methods available which cover the most important aspects of water chemistry. But most aquarists will probably prefer to use the tried method of changing a portion of the tank water every two to three months. In spite of careful cleaning there will always be hidden corners in which particles of dirt accumulate and form a

To protect the tank from possible pollution it is best to first rinse well live foods like the *Tubifex* worms shown here.   Photo by Dr. H. R. Axelrod.

deposit of detritus. These can be quite easily siphoned off before they have a chance to decompose and foul the water.

Fish, like humans, have to work for their daily food. The exact rules governing this continual struggle are not always understood, but there is no doubt that the strongest and most aggressive always gets the biggest helping. This tendency can, and must, be counteracted by judicious selection of species when the aquarium is first stocked and by suitable feeding. One so often hears or reads about the 'food problem.' In my view the aquarist of today has no food problem, except perhaps in the case of a very few specialized feeders. The extensive menu includes *Daphnia, Cyclops,* midge and fly larvae, whiteworms, *Tubifex* and a number of good dried foods which are enriched with vitamins. Some fish are rather fussy feeders, for they often show a preference for certain kinds of food. Nevertheless, with time and patience it is usually possible to get most fish to eat food that was at first refused. In general, I believe that it is important to pay attention to the normal feeding habits of the different species. A bottom-feeding fish would need to be very hungry to take its food in open water. Such animals will only leave the bottom very unwillingly to feed. In fact there are even fish which would rather starve than feed in a way that is not in accordance with their normal habits.

Surface-feeding wrestling half-beaks, *Dermogenys pusillus*, feed mostly on live insects which are scooped up by the half-beaks' uniquely formed mouth parts. Photo by Chvojka Milan.

Plants fulfill several functions including serving as spawning sites for many free-spawning fishes like the flame tetra, *Hyphessobrycon flammeus*, shown here. To some extent the eggs escape predation also. Photo by R. Zukal.

Aquarium fish are mostly peaceful animals whose best methods of defense are flight, concealment and camouflage. Free-swimming fish should therefore have sufficient space for escape, and for many species it is essential to provide hiding-places under rocks and roots or in plant thickets. In an aquarium where no attention is paid to such requirements one must expect that the fish will always be relatively shy and, quite understandably, aggressive.

An aquarium should house aquatic plants for both biological and aesthetic reasons. Plants help to keep the water clean, they offer shelter to the fish and their leaves and stems are used as spawning sites by those which lay sticky eggs. In addition, of course, they give off oxygen and absorb carbon dioxide during the process of photosynthesis, and this is of great value to an aquarium. Their aesthetic value is just as great, unless the aquarium is to be regarded merely as a container for breeding fish.

There are certain plants which only attain their full beauty when they are grown as single specimens. Others give of their best when planted in a group with others of their kind. One can, therefore, produce a thick growth of vegetation on the bottom, leaving the water above free of plants, or one can have long-stalked leafy plants producing a surface cover, but leaving the underlying water free. Aquatic plants will certainly grow in artificial light, although certain aquarists still believe that they require some daylight. It is true that our knowledge in this field is still rather sketchy, but results with artificial light are very encouraging. The lighting industry has made great efforts to produce lamps which will promote growth, and the outlook is promising. Although these developments are mainly intended for horticultural and biological research, the aquarist can also profit from them. This is a field in which it would pay to experiment.

Aquatic plants take in nutrients either through the roots or through the leaves. Some use both methods. Apart from floating plants they all require a substrate of sand or gravel for anchorage. They will only develop a healthy root system if the substrate contains sufficient nutrient and if its particles are of the correct size. It should be possible for water to flow through the whole substrate, to prevent the formation of areas of decomposition. Artificial fertilizers can be used when the natural store of nutrient becomes insufficient to support the plants.

The most important accessory in the aquarium is the aquarist himself. Anyone who wants to install an aquarium as a form of decoration or relaxation should have the services of a professional aquarist, unless he is able to do the job himself.

2.

Suggested Designs

Sometimes my hair stands on end when I see certain aquaria which are intended as room decoration; a fish cage, garnished with innumerable inlet and outlet tubes, cables along the sides and on the bottom, filter beds hanging on by rusty hoops and a switchboard suitable for a medium-sized power station. In short, the whole thing is a confused jumble. It has as little to do with room decoration as technology has with beauty. Fortunately there are exceptions and sometimes one comes across the work of a real individualist.

The other extreme has just as little to recommend it. An aquarium tank built into a bar is harmless compared with some of the ideas thought up by clever businessmen, such as overdecorated indoor fountains with fish and underwater lighting, aquaria installed under glass table-tops or glass vases housing a few fish in their bases.

In fact it is not so easy as it might appear to make an aquarium fit harmoniously into the decor of a room, but this it must do whether it is intended to be the main feature in an ultra-modern interior design, to enliven the cozy atmosphere of a living-room or perhaps to make an office a little less forbidding. An aquarium tank will always be an eyecatcher because of the contrast between its contents and its surroundings. It would be a mistake to install such an unusual form of decoration alongside a particularly attractive and striking wall. The same applies to the opposite extreme, as when someone tries to camouflage a tank in a piece of special furniture. Naturally one must differentiate between designing an aquarium for a completely new building and trying to fit one into an existing home. In the first place the proportions of the tank play an important role. All the relevant technical problems must be carefully thought out before work starts. When installing an aquarium in an existing room the size and shape of the tank are usually dictated by the other elements in the room.

Other difficulties may arise in relation to the positioning of the tank. It is bad enough to spill a glass of beer in a restaurant and damage a table or chair, but it is infinitely worse if the beer goes into an aquarium where it will cause torture to the animals. So it is better to keep tanks in such places properly covered. Local temperature changes also play a considerable role. A check should be kept on this, because trouble may arise in a room where the temperature fluctuates grossly. This is because aquarium heaters only cover a restricted range and both fish and plants are sensitive to big temperature fluctuations. As we have already seen daylight is not indispensable.

Aquaria can, of course, be insured. Nevertheless it is not pleasant when an aquarium glass cracks. This may occur, for example, in the vicinity of a factory or a railway where slight vibration is taking place all the time.

Aquarium fish may indeed become good pets, but just as they do not drink beer, so also they should not be subjected to the effects of nicotine. Care should therefore be taken to ensure that air loaded with tobacco smoke or other impurities does not reach the tank. The compressed air supply can be cleaned by passing it through a wash-bottle.

Like a picture on the wall

The idea of installing an aquarium in a hole in the wall is not new. This allows the observer to see only the front

An aquarium set behind a wall opening.

of the tank, the remainder of which butts into a side-room. This can be an advantage in places where there is not enough space to allow the whole tank to be accommodated inside the room. In addition it allows all the technical equipment to be concealed in the side room. The hole in the wall can be framed with timber or with natural or artificial rockwork, or it can be simply left smooth. Whichever method is used the length and the height of the hole in the wall should be 1-2 inches less than the length and height of the tank so that only the front glass and none of the frame is visible. The actual height of the tank above the floor will depend upon whether you are going to look at it from a sitting or standing position. Beneath the tank, and perhaps to one side, one can place a decorative house-plant, such as a good specimen of *Monstera*. Anyone who finds that an asbestos cement tank appears too ponderous could well use this method of insetting in a wall and at the same time enjoy the technical advantages.

Made of cement

Naturally an aquarium tank can also be made of cement, provided the floor is sufficiently strong to bear it. Indeed, such an aquarium is the dream of many aquarists, as it has several advantages and offers opportunities for experiment. It can, for example, have built-in filter chambers or be fitted with a drainage system to allow easy emptying (this is a great advantage when a thorough cleaning is necessary). In special cases, as for example in marine aquaria, a cement tank will be found convenient for the installation of permanent rockwork.

The aquarist can of course build such a cement tank himself, but it is usually advisable to call in an expert, so as to avoid problems due to the great weight. Cement aquaria must undergo thorough treatment before being used. Cement gives off substances producing hardness and in some circumstances may be poisonous. The cement can usually be rendered safe by thoroughly brushing with a weak acid solution (5-10%), followed by rinsing for some days in running water and a repetition of the whole process. To be really safe it is best to follow this treatment by coating the inside of the tank with a silicon rubber compound or with an epoxy resin. If delicate or expensive animals are to be kept in such a tank it is advisable to obtain a water analysis from a chemical laboratory after the water has been in continuous circulation for several days.

The installation of lights for a cement aquarium is very simple; fluorescent tubes with reflectors can simply be suspended from the ceiling. The number and wattage of the lamps will depend upon the size of the tank. If several tubes are used one has a chance to experiment with light of different wave-lengths. It is obvious that the tank cover must be of glass or translucent plastic. The lamps should be suspended just above the cover as the

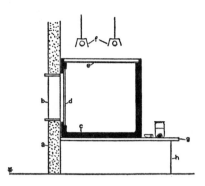

Diagram of a cement tank set behind a wall opening. a = wall, b = hole in wall, c = cement tank in section, d = aquarium glass, e = tank cover, f = lights, g = tank base, h = supporting base.

light intensity decreases with the square of the distance, and plenty of light will be needed. The tank can also be illuminated by underwater lamps. These have watertight fittings and usually also a reflector, but the range of wavelengths available is limited, so one cannot experiment very much. It is also a little difficult to replace the tubes. The term 'underwater lamp' does not mean that these fittings must always be submerged. They can be used just as well above the water surface and under the tank cover, or in any position where the air is very humid. If underwater lamps are used they should be placed under the tank cover or in the water because otherwise it would not really pay to install them. The cover can then be made of a material that is not translucent, but never of metal or any other substance that will be damaged by humidity. Asbestos cement sheets are very suitable for this, and more will be said later about their use in the aquarium.

A small rebate or step round the upper edge of the cement tank will provide support for the cover and also prevent condensation from dripping down outside the tank. As already mentioned, an aquarium tank placed behind a wall is very suitable for experimental purposes, and it allows all the technical equipment to be kept out of sight.

Tanks reinforced with stainless steel frames are strong and can be used for marine fishes provided the direct contact between the salt water and the metal is prevented. The upper edges of the tank can be coated with silicon rubber sealer which acts as a barrier between the water and the metal; all internal joints also must be sealed. Photo by Dr. H. R. Axelrod.

This kind of installation would be very suitable for a doctor who has a waiting-room with an adjoining side-room, and who is also an experimentally minded aquarist. What is more natural than to combine the attractive with something practical and—if space allows—to make the aquarium visible to the patients by means of a hole in the waiting-room wall. Nowadays many doctors appreciate the relaxing and restful effect of an aquarium tank on waiting patients. This is easily understandable, particularly in an urban practice, where people come in from the everyday strains of a modern city. A relaxed patient also eases the job of the harassed general practitioner. Behind the wall the doctor can turn aquarist in his spare time and do a little tidying up.

In recent years all-glass tanks have become very popular. On the whole the results are satisfying. There is a

When made from the proper type of glass an all-glass tank is recommended. It allows the maximum exposure of the contents to view and is the best for marine fishes, as poisoning from metal corrosion is completely eliminated.

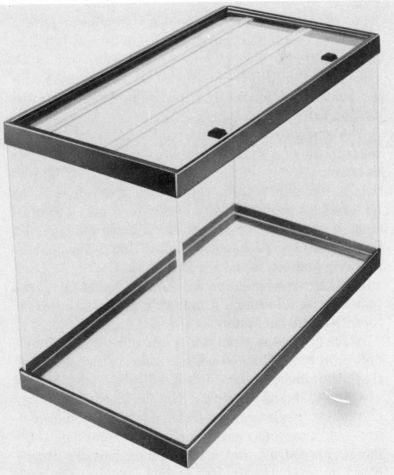

problem in the construction of frameless plastic aquaria. Here, however, it is the danger that the sheets may bend outwards if the tank is large. In addition, thin plastic becomes somewhat distorted under the influence of humidity and heat. It can stand a small amount of warmth, but not real heat. Nevertheless there is no doubt that in the course of time transparent plastic will become more widely used in a number of different aquarium techniques.

Some general considerations

It seems that certain psychological moments play a significant role in the field of aquarium design. Whether one should also draw practical conclusions from such reflections I must leave undecided. In any case the subject seems to be sufficiently attractive to permit some discussion here.

The tendency of modern architecture is to open up the frontage of a shop and by the use of plenty of glass to enable the man in the street to look at everything in detail, sometimes from more than one angle. This increases his confidence and his desire to buy. The principle of offering every conceivable type of merchandise in transparent packages achieves the same object. Modern man is accustomed, or encouraged, to react strongly to visual impressions. An aquarium that allows him to walk all around it and look in from all sides is thus a modern aquarium.

In the past many government and other official buildings have been designed with a mass of fussy detail, so that the ordinary citizen finds it difficult to take them in as a whole, and he is perplexed by the maze of corridors and offices. He becomes somewhat uncertain and helpless and is only too easily inclined to view the whole thing with distrust. But such organizations are usually based on trust. The modern architect tries to give such

A specially built 60-gallon hexagonal tank which permits viewing into the tank not only on all sides but also at the top. Photo by A. F. Orsini.

buildings an air of openness by the use of clean lines and simple shapes. Faced with the problem of planning an aquarium for such a building it is obvious that here too one should work on the open-plan principle and have the tank standing free and visible from all around.

Even today the profession of medicine is in some ways surrounded with an aura of secrecy. Is it not true that, in spite of progress and explanation, modern man still connects his search for a cure with a certain belief in miracles?

The patient in the waiting-room expects unknown apparatus and smells, rare and incomprehensible manipulation, earnest, searching looks and friendly encouragement. The waiting-room cannot help having this aura. So why not agree on this point and install an aquarium which will have a slight air of secrecy? Let the observer see only a living picture, but keep the works hidden from him.

In planning an aquarium as a showpiece, schools and colleges employ other quite different considerations. On the one hand, they are concerned here with a critical, modern public dedicated to finding out about things. On the other hand, the installation must be designed in such a way as to stimulate the observation of nature. So here they should make visible as many as possible of the numerous interlocking and overlapping biological processes. I believe that in such circumstances a combination of an aquarium and a rain-forest vivarium (paludarium) might provide a useful and stimulating solution to the problem. This could pass from a purely aquatic part with fish and plants into a shoreline with stones and roots for amphibious animals. One would need to ensure that good marsh plants could be grown and that the whole was rounded off with a small greenhouse roof of epiphytic rain-forest plants. This would give a living community which could offer a really broad field for observation.

How to set about it

Free standing aquaria are usually only seen at their best in large spaces. This type of aquarium is very suitable for entrance halls and similar spaces in official buildings, but it raises a number of problems. All the technical equipment must be placed above the tank instead of being hidden away behind the side or back walls. It would not be sensible to put this gear beneath the tank, because the lighting has to be above and the filter, if external, ought not to be at a lower level than the surface

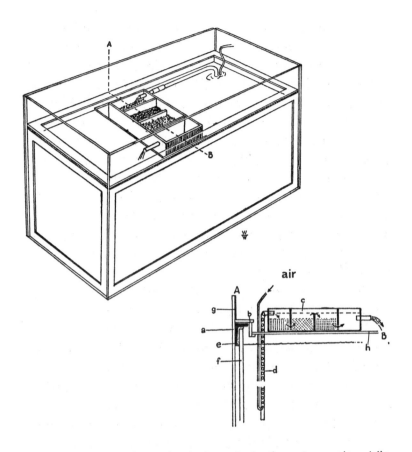

Chambered filter above the tank and plastic outer casing (diagrammatic). A–B = section through the chambered filter, a = plastic outer casing, b = bracing piece acting as support for tank cover, c = chambered filter, d = air-lift to filter, e = angle-iron of tank, f = front glass, g = screen to shield lights and conceal equipment, h = tank cover.

of the water. So such a filter would need to be raised above the tank. It could in fact only be placed beneath the tank if one were using a closed, watertight circulation. But this would be so complicated and difficult to service that it is not worth considering. The usual method is to use a series of filters and different layers of filtration media, such as gravel, charcoal, nylon, etc. There are two ways in which this type of filter could be connected to a free-standing tank. First, we could install a flat filter chamber above the center of the tank, with the individual compartments lying alongside each other. The water would be brought to the filter by a circulating pump or by a vibrating diaphragm pump and air-lift. This method is reliable, provided the rate of flow is correlated with the dimensions of the filter. This type of filter is easy to clean and maintain. The tank is illuminated by fluorescent tubes suspended from above and protected against spray. The lights should be fixed in such a way that they can be moved upwards or sideways to facilitate servicing.

The second solution of the problem requires the installation of a tree trunk complete with its main roots in one corner of the tank. The trunk rises at least 2 inches above the surface of the water in the tank and houses a plastic filter inside its hollow interior. The tank water enters the tree trunk at its base, rises toward the surface and spills over into the inner, cylindrical filter. The water is sucked through the filter layers by a circulating pump or by a vibrating diaphragm pump. Heaters and thermostats and their cables can be concealed in one corner of the tank.

The external appearance of such an installation will be much influenced by the open view from all sides. There is really no need to cover the outside of the aquarium frame; a suitable coat of paint would be sufficient. But there will need to be a lid to hide the filter and the lamps. It would probably be best to paint the frame the same color as the screen shielding the technical equipment. To obtain a clean, modern facing, first paint the iron frame with a plastic resin of a neutral color. Then place sheets of transparent plastic across each side of the tank and glue them to the frame, making sure

Diagram of a filter built into a tree trunk. a = tree (alternatively rock or coral), b = water rising to filter, c = filter, d = submerged circulating pump, e = water level.

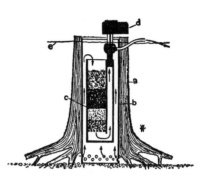

that each sheet joins flush with its neighbor. This not only provides a clean-lined modern facing but also gives the effect of double glazing and thus helps to prevent heat loss. This job must be done in a cool, dry room. The external transparent facing should rise to a height just a little greater than that of the technical equipment and should be stabilized by cross-struts of plastic; these strips also serve to support the tank cover. This edging of plastic above the tank can be darkened either with colored plastic sheets or by simply painting it; it will then shield the lamps and hide the technical equipment. If the tank is not too large, the whole outer covering of plastic can be made in one piece and be removable. This would have the advantage of allowing the inner glass to be cleaned.

The completed tank rests on a solid base strong enough to take the weight. This could be made of stout timber or as a welded metal frame. Naturally it would be even better, if local conditions allow, to make the base of brick or cement, to give the impression of stability and solidity. In other words the base should appear more stable than the load it has to carry. If attention is not paid to this point, the whole set-up will appear top-heavy and unattractive. The top of the base on which the tank is to rest should be a strong plank of wood, or a slab of stone or artificial rock. If wood is used it should be coated above and along the edges with a water-repelling paint, preferably an epoxy resin, for there will always be drops of water in the vicinity of any aquarium. If possible the base plate should project about 4 inches all round to provide a ledge. The hollow interior of the base could well serve as a cupboard in which to store nets and other equipment, switches for the electrical gear, chokes for the fluorescent lamps, small tanks with live food, fish medicines and chemicals. Obviously this cupboard must be kept locked if the public are admitted.

A free-standing aquarium.

Aquarium forming a partition wall.

An aquarium as a partition wall

A tank of the type just described can also be set with one of its short sides butting onto a wall, and if large enough it will then serve as a partition. This would accord with the modern trend towards open-plan rooms with half partitions, which are often used as book-cases or plant stands. So why not have an aquarium?

This principle can be used to provide semi-private alcoves in restaurants or to divide up very long rooms so that part of the space is shielded from view.

With the aquarium tank positioned in this way some of the technical equipment may have to be rearranged. For example, a suitable space left between the wall and the end of the aquarium could be enclosed to form a cupboard. This could house a fairly large external filter, which would be easily accessible. The interior decoration of such a tank should not be based on a central focal point. It would be better to cover the end near the wall to represent, for example, a shore zone.

27

Tanks in a corner

The serious aquarist is not usually satisfied by a single tank. So why not have two matching tanks set in a corner of the room?

This would allow him to have, say, two species of fish from the same habitat, which could not be kept together in captivity. In such a case the two closely adjacent tanks could be decorated so as to suggest that they were actually one. Or they could, of course, be furnished in contrasting styles.

Two aquarium tanks arranged in this way always look good and there are also a number of technical advantages. Take for example the aquarist who is interested in large cichlids or other sizeable fish that burrow in the

Aquaria in a corner.

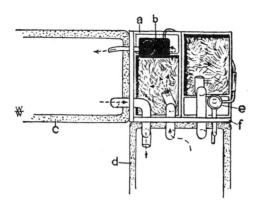

Filter arrangement for two tanks set in a corner (*seen from above:* the arrows show the direction of flow through the filter and both tanks), a = filter box, b = submerged circulation pump in the post-filter chamber (clear water), c and d = the two tanks, e = second filter driven by diaphragm pump for independent filtration of one tank, f = wooden box with holes for the tubing.

substrate and destroy the vegetation. Now plants are, of course, biologically very important in a freshwater aquarium. The answer to this problem is to stock the second tank with small, peaceful fish and some attractive plants, to light it in the same way and to arrange for it to share filtration and circulation with the first tank. To do this, the two tanks should have the same height and breadth, but the lengths can differ. The space left in the corner between the two tanks will provide an excellent home for the filtration plant.

Even if both tanks normally share a common filter, provision should be made for each to have its own filter. There is, in fact, plenty of room for two filters in the available space. The arrangement could be roughly on the following lines. A wooden box should be made to fit exactly in the space between the two tanks. The two walls of the box adjoining the tank ends should be as

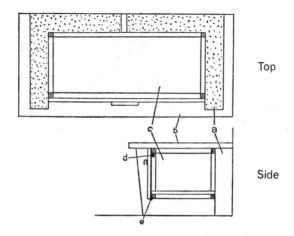

Top

Side

Diagram of a cement base. a = L-shaped cement section, b = base plate for the tank, c = built-in cupboard, d = door with magnetic catch, e = hinge.

high as the strip used to mask the lamps; they will need to be quite high if floating plants are grown. Naturally the two high walls must be properly painted to prevent them warping or rotting. These walls are then drilled to take the necessary inlet and outlet tubes, and they will also serve to take fixings for part of the front screen. The lamps can either be attached to the inside of the screen or they can be suspended from the underside of the tank cover. To provide stability, a quarter or a third of the rear part of each tank cover can be fixed to the frame of the screen and the front part made to open (using plastic hinges). The filter is closed above by a loose top.

The tank base can be made of two L-shaped pieces of cast cement, covered with a slab to bear the weight of the tank, the front remaining open. The free space beneath the slab can be made into a cupboard, with a door opening downwards, which is closed by a magnetic catch. The cupboard should not reach to the floor otherwise cleaning will be impossible. The cement base can be finished with a rendering of rough cement or with strips of suitable timber. The great advantage of this type is that it can easily be removed if necessary.

Tall aquaria

In aquarium and vivarium work it is always a good plan to bear in mind the educational needs of young people and to present to them biological processes or concepts as a means of arousing their interest. An aquarium by itself can only achieve this to a limited extent, but we can go further by providing an aqua-vivarium or aqua-paludarium. This can take the form of a relatively tall tank in which the bottom layer or ground floor contains fish and rooted aquatic plants. The first floor can be a rocky shoreline rising above the water surface and planted with tropical marsh plants, where amphibians can walk about. This floor would also have the emersed

A paludarium installed in an entrance hall.

parts of the water plants. The second floor can be a somewhat drier piece of land, planted with tropical ground plants, including perhaps a few terrestrial orchids. Finally the third floor, just below the tank cover, can house one or two tree branches with epiphytic plants.

This type of aqua-vivarium provides rich opportunities for observing the interrelationships between land and water, between plants and animals and so on. I believe that this kind of arrangement would be particularly suitable for schools.

Naturally the technical problems involved are somewhat greater than in an ordinary aquarium. The observer must have an uninterrupted view of the whole exhibit, so the glass front should not be subdivided into panes. The area of glass above the water must be kept free from condensation. The tank must be ventilated with fresh air at a constant and correct temperature. The lighting must provide good illumination from the bottom layer with aquatic plants up to the tree zone with epiphytes, and yet must not appear glaring. The whole installation must be protected against humidity and be easily serviceable from one side.

Unfortunately the glass panes of paludaria become 'steamed up' when the temperature outside the tank is lower than that of the moisture-saturated space inside. This can be overcome in the following way. A second, relatively thin pane of glass is fixed—in a channel—in front of the main pane, leaving a gap of about ½ inch between the two. A tube, closed at one end, is laid along the bottom of this air gap. The upper side of the tube is pierced by a series of holes, the total area of which should correspond approximately to the bore of the tube. Some or all of the switch gear serving the tank is installed in a box which should be made as airtight as possible. Air from a vibrating diaphragm pump is led

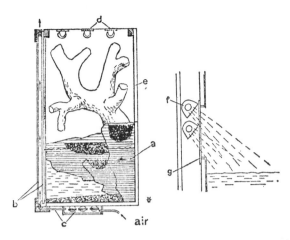

Diagram of paludarium from side. a = land area decoration, b = inner and outer glass panes enclosing stream of warm air, c = provision of warm air and switch gear, d = overhead lights, e = rear wall (removable part), f = side lights, g = glass in front of side lights.

into this box, where it is warmed by the switch gear. The warm air is then led by as short a tube as possible (to prevent heat loss) to the horizontal tubing lying between the two glass panes. There the air leaves the tube and warms the two panes of glass as it rises. The incidental cooling of the switch gear is an additional advantage. It should, however, be stressed that the diaphragm pump must always be switched on at the same time as the lighting, otherwise the switch gear in the enclosed box will suffer damage. It is obvious that there must be a series of holes at the top of the air space to allow the warm air to escape.

The ordinary aquarium aerator will provide a steady supply of fresh air to the aerial parts of the tank. Some tropical plants and vivarium animals are very sensitive to big fluctuations in humidity, but these can be avoided by installing a system of ventilation controlled by a hygrostat.

The proportion of water to air can be in the ratio of 1:3 to 1:4 (e.g. 18 inches water in a total height of 6 feet).

The construction of the shore part should present no great difficulty. The rockwork can be built up of carefully selected stones, and it is simpler to do this before the front glass is fitted. The stones or rocks are fixed together with Silastic silicone cement. The submerged

The newt *Triturus vulgaris* is an ideal animal to keep in an aquarium-vivarium set-up. As an amphibian it can get in and out of the water according to its physiological requirements. Photo by L. E. Perkins.

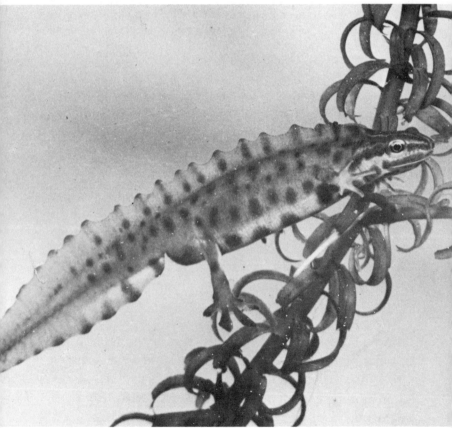

A well-balanced paludarium set up like this will require the removal of excess growth regularly in order to preserve the original appearance. Plant growth can also be limited by regulating the amount of light. Photo by L. E. Perkins.

parts should merge gradually with the parts above the water surface. Any spaces that are left, which might become filled with plant detritus, should be filled in with a mixture of polyester resin and naturally colored stone chips or fine sand. Large holes should first be filled with gravel and then covered over with this mixture. This job should be done quickly because the polyester resin hardens very rapidly. It is always best to mix only a part of the total quantity required. A hole should be left at a suitable place in the land area to accommodate the branch that will support the epiphytes. The remainder of the submerged part can be regarded as an ordinary aquarium. The selection and arrangement of the different aquatic and marsh plants must remain a matter for individual taste, taking into account the light and other requirements of the individual species. The aquarium part can be stocked with Archer Fish, Spraying Characins and similar fish, supplemented by newts, ornamental terrapins, aquatic frogs and tree frogs.

Sufficient fluorescent tubes should be installed to allow a certain amount of experimentation. Unfortunately daylight raises a number of problems. As we know, terrestrial plants can do with all the daylight they can get, but in the aquatic part of the tank, floating algae will soon gain the upper hand if there is too much daylight. Therefore it is advisable not to place such an aquavivarium close to a window. The amount of artificial illumination should be sufficient to light the whole tank without recourse to daylight. It is much simpler to install an adequate number of lamps at the start than to try squeezing in additional ones at a later stage.

Once again, the tank should have a stable and practical base, and it might also be aesthetically attractive to place the whole installation between two square pillars.

A series of tanks

In some circumstances a series of long, relatively shallow tanks can be aesthetically satisfying. The particular appeal of such an arrangement lies in the possibilities the length provides for decorative treatment. For instance I would suggest that the short side of a room could be made very attractive by installing three tanks, each the same height and length, stretching from wall to wall. They will look well if painted white and positioned in front of a bottle-green wall, at a height suitable for armchair viewing.

The lamps can be the usual fluorescent trough fittings. If they are shielded by beaten copper sheet they will blend in harmoniously with the background wall. Each tank should be lit by a single lamp suspended by two

Three tanks running from wall to wall.

cords. The lamps must be capable of being raised or moved out of the way when the tank is being serviced. If more light is needed, one can use the type of fitting that takes two fluorescent tubes.

The tanks can rest on a long, continuous slab supported on brackets firmly embedded in the wall. Or they can be placed on a base made of stable rigid prefabricated units, arranged so that some are open at the front and others closed to form small cupboards. This is very practical, for it gives storage space for books, equipment and so on, but aesthetically it is not so pleasing as the first method.

In this type of installation there is no space for an outside filter either at the back or sides, so only an internal filter can be used.

In my opinion the three tanks should be decorated as a single unit. They could, for instance, represent the cross-section of a stream. Starting on the left, there is a sloping shore with roots and rocks leading gradually to the middle of the stream (center tank). The right hand tank has a slight dip in the bottom with two or three rocks, in the lee of which a group of plants has taken root. The ground then rises to the shoreline on the extreme right. Fish from the same natural habitat are now distributed among the tanks in such a way that shy species which prefer to live among plants are put into the shore zone tanks, while free-swimming fish are housed in the center tank; this can also have bottom-living species which will soon find a home under the large flat rocks in the middle of the stream.

An aquarium cupboard

Serious aquarists often become caught up in the scientific aspects of their subject. This is quite understandable. If we are quite honest, we must confess that our interest in aquaria is largely a matter of curiosity. We want to get to know this or that animal in its natural environment, and to observe it feeding, fighting and courting. When the aquarist suddenly feels an urge to extend his observations beyond the realm of every-day events, to enter fields where information is lacking or sparse, he is still far from being a scientist, but he will acquire a certain scientific approach.

For comparative observations it is usual to set up a number of similar tanks. There are few people who have unlimited space at their disposal for such an installation. Often the work has to be carried out in a single room, but of course this makes comparisons easier.

Such an extensive installation would dominate a living-room and appear oppressive. This has given me

Modern aquarium cupboard.

the idea of having the tanks hidden away in a special piece of furniture.

I would devote the short wall of a room to this purpose, and suggest that the tanks should be accommodated in a specially fitted cupboard. Let us assume that we have to provide for nine equal-sized tanks, in three rows of three. Aquaria for research purposes need not be enormous. It would be reasonable for each tank to have a capacity of about 20 gallons. Let us therefore decide on tanks 24 inches long, 15 inches broad and 12 inches deep, and reckon on a total weight of about 2,000 pounds. So it is quite essential to make sure that the floor can carry this weight.

We do not usually look at aquaria from the viewpoint of weight, but here the structure must be stable, yet built in such a way that it does not appear clumsy. It should, if possible, be made in the style of a modern cupboard. The main load is carried by the horizontal supports beneath the tanks. In the present case we use timber cross-members set on edge. It is well known that a solid vertical timber wall will carry heavy loads, even if quite thin, provided that it is firmly fixed and truly vertical.

The side walls and the two vertical partition walls are made of good timber planks. At the appropriate heights, two cross-members run from one side wall to the other, passing through the two partition walls. They are firmly fixed to the side walls. The total height of the whole cupboard is made up of the height of the bottom cross-member, the thickness of a plywood sheet, the height of the tank standing on it plus the free space between the top of the tank and the next cross-member (about 12 inches), and so on to the roof of the cupboard. The front cross-member occupies the first third of the distance between the front and back of the cupboard. There should also be a strong cross-member just below the roof of the cupboard. The back is formed by a rigid frame with vertical strips to which the rear cross-members are fixed. The open space above each tank should be screened off by a mask that opens upwards. Finally, each tank compartment has a sliding door. The whole of the front can be closed by these doors or individual doors can be slid behind their neighbors. The runners of the sliding doors are provided with catches, so that the individual doors can be removed if one wishes to watch all three tanks in a horizontal row at the same time. When all the doors are closed the whole piece of furniture looks like a subdivided cupboard. A great advantage of the sliding doors is that one can, if necessary, observe one or more tanks undisturbed, while the others remain hidden.

The compartments in which the tanks stand are best lined with PVC which should be properly glued in the corners, to protect the timber against humidity. The whole installation can be provided with a single air compressor or each tank can have its own submerged circulating pump. In any case the air lines and other tubes should be neatly installed and provided with taps and connections for each tank. Ventilation slits should be provided to allow adequate renewal of the air above each tank. The lamps can be fitted between the two cross-members, where they will not be in the way during servicing. Finally the front and sides of the cupboard and the vertical partitions should be finished in a pale timber and the sliding doors covered with an attractive dark veneer that will match the neighboring furniture. The aquarist will then have a piece that can be put into any living-room without appearing out of place.

Small but good

I have quite deliberately left the instructions for designing a small individual aquarium to the end of this chapter, although from its nature this type of tank might really have belonged at the beginning. But I believe that this widespread and popular aquarium is best suited to complete the series.

This kind of tank is suitable for the son to satisfy his newly aroused interest in keeping animals, for the father whose job leaves him little time for bigger things and for the grandfather who has resumed his childhood dreams and now needs some variety in his later years.

This is not a large aquarium, but it should have a special place in the room, where it will act as counterpart to a bird cage or to a window-sill with potted plants.

Small aquarium as part of book case.

It will adorn the base of any piece of furniture. Often, however, it is put in the wrong position in a room, in an endeavor to put it in the right light, and it may then appear quite out of place. Nevertheless, it is not really so difficult, even with relatively limited means to fit this kind of aquarium into a home. The following examples, which can be varied at will, are intended to act as a stimulus.

Modern book units, with a U-shaped cross-section, are now widely available. They can be placed alongside each other and will even fit into a corner. It would be quite feasible to install a small aquarium as an integral part of a group of these book units. The tank is exactly the same height and depth as each individual unit. A metal angle section, almost as long as the tank and strong enough to bear its weight, is firmly screwed to the wall. This is the support for the aquarium. A book unit abuts each end of the tank, but it is best not to fit the aquarium right in the middle of a wall.

The frame of the tank is, of course, painted the same color as the book units, unless you use an all-glass tank.

It is advisable to mask the front of the tank to prevent light from escaping. The tank should be covered with a lid of the same color as the neighboring paint, to give a flush surface. A submerged circulating pump or a vibrating diaphragm pump can be placed in one of the neighboring book units and hidden by a few sham book fronts.

As an alternative to this suggestion, the aquarium can be placed in association with a couple of ordinary book shelves.

An aquarium near the window-sill.

Here the weight is taken by two tall forks of timber braced at the bottom by cross-pieces, so that each resembles an elongated A. At the base the two sides are joined by cross-members on which the timber-clad tank is placed. The lid, or part of it, is made to open.

The tank could, of course, be put directly on the cross-members, omitting the external covering. But the timber gives an attractive appearance and, being fixed to the side pieces, it also helps to stabilize the whole structure. Two or three plain book shelves can then be fixed above the tank. The whole unit could be used to divide a room or simply be placed against a wall.

Combined aquarium and book rack.

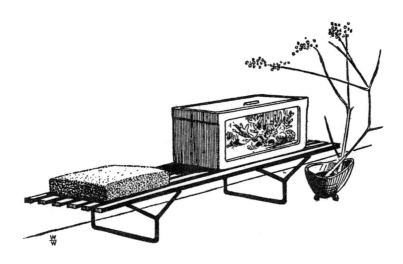

An aquarium as part of
a small decorative scheme.

A further alternative is to place the aquarium on a window-sill, but in practice this is not really a good idea. Tanks exposed to too much direct sunlight frequently suffer from a plague of algae, and once a 'water bloom' has become established, nothing else will be seen. Furthermore, there is little pleasure in always viewing the fish and plants in transmitted light. So I recommend that the tank should be set at right angles to the window, jutting out into the room.

Here the tank rests on a slab of the same material as the sill, supported by a strong base. The aquarium then stands near the window and is architecturally related to the sill. It is no longer viewed by transmitted light and yet it receives adequate illumination. Nevertheless, provision should be made to light the tank by submerged lamps or by overhead fluorescent tubes in trough fittings. The aquarium is not clad externally, but is neatly painted and given a few house plants in the vicinity.

3.

Materials

There is scarcely any other hobby which is dependent upon such a large number of good materials as aquariology. The efficient aquarist is constantly seeking for new materials in order to test whether they are suitable for his purpose.

The materials used in aquaria must not only be resistant to oxidation and putrefaction, but it is essential that they should not release any soluble toxic substances into the water.

Glass

On account of its transparency, glass is naturally the most important material used in the aquarium.

Even top quality glass has occasional defects. Unfortunately these are often not noticed at the time of purchase, but may become very obvious when the tank is completed.

In spite of the apparent hardness of a sheet of glass it should never be handled roughly when being polished, as it easily becomes scratched. This is very annoying when watching the fish.

Sealers

It is not so easy to find a really good aquarium sealer. On the one hand it must be strong enough to fasten the glass to the frame, but not too stiff, and it should yield

Some African cichlids in a tank with rockwork arranged in a way similar to the rocky shores of Lake Malawi. These fishes are very territorial, as indicated here by a male *Pseudotropheus auratus* inside "his" cave. Photo by R. Zukal.

to the water pressure. On the other hand it must be capable of preventing the water from leaking out of the tank. All aquarium cements based on linseed oil dry out sooner or later and become hard and friable, so that splits appear and leaks start.

For some years plastic sealers have been on the market and these are exceedingly adhesive. They are scarcely capable of drying out and they are very elastic. These substances are very suitable for aquaria and they are only slightly more expensive than the ordinary cements. Silicone-based cements are available everywhere.

Cement

Cement is used not only in the construction of tank bases, but is sometimes also needed for decorative purposes. However, its use in the aquarium always raises some problems. But the substitutes for cement are all considerably more expensive. So one usually has to fall back on cement, at least for decorating marine tanks. Skilled aquarists create completely natural rocky backgrounds out of glass-wool impregnated with cement, in the same way as model railways are embellished with hills and rocks made out of size and crumpled paper.

Some cements contain toxic substances and these should be rejected, and over a period of time all cements give off substances producing water hardness.

Such injurious substances must as far as possible be removed from the cement. This can be done by alternately painting the inside of the tank with dilute hydrochloric acid and rinsing with running water. This should be repeated several times, and the tank will then be safe.

In constructing tank bases out of cement, care should be taken to ensure that the dimensions and strength are adequate to support the weight of the tank, and also that the floor of the room is sufficiently strong. In case of doubt it would be best to seek professional advice.

Rockwork

Rocks form an important part of the decoration, but not all kinds of rock are suitable. Calcareous rocks produce an increase in the hardness of the water and are therefore undesirable in a freshwater aquarium. This is a great pity because some rocks in this group, e.g. dolomite, are quite bizarre and very decorative. In marine aquaria, on the other hand, these rocks are perfectly safe, as here the hardness produced is of no importance.

There are, however, plenty of other rocks which can be used in freshwater tanks, as for example the various igneous rocks, sandstone and slate. These points naturally apply also to the substrate. Here again one should only use sand that is free of calcium. If in doubt the sand should be tested with hydrochloric acid: calcareous matter foams when a few drops of acid are poured on it.

It is very important to include at least one smooth flat stone for spawning substrate brooders like the African cichlid *Pelmatochromis thomasi* pictured here. The nesting site is defended for some time until the young are free-swimming. Photo by R. Zukal.

Various metals are known to be toxic in the aquarium, and so any rocks that are suspected of containing metals should be rejected. The sand for the substrate should, so far as possible, be smooth with roundish grains to avoid damage to fish that burrow in the bottom. Gravel from dark igneous rocks is intended for use as road-bed and it is broken up into sharp-edged pieces. Nevertheless a dark substrate is very decorative, and the aquarist may be fortunate enough to find some dark, round-grained gravel in, say, the bed of a mountain stream.

An aquarium set-up with artificial and natural decorations tastefully combined against a substrate of dark coarse gravel. Whatever kinds of decorations and bottom are chosen, it is imperative to examine them very closely for possible toxicity. They can be tested by using a few inexpensive fishes prior to introducing the fishes intended to be kept in the tank. Photo by Dr. H. R. Axelrod.

Lava stone is igneous in origin and can be installed with confidence in a freshwater tank provided that it does not contain too many cavities in which organic matter could decompose. Photo by G. J. M. Timmerman.

Glues

The glues used in aquarium work must also fulfil strict requirements. They must naturally withstand normal tensions, but must also be unaffected by fresh and sea water over long periods of time. Most of the modern glues appear to be perfectly satisfactory. Unfortunately the price increases with the quality. When properly used the silicone glues are almost ideal adhesives for aquarium work. They can be used, for example, to stick together the constituent parts of quite large decorative rockwork backgrounds. Usually such structures appear somewhat disjointed when first assembled. If this is so, one can make a paste of polyester resin mixed with fine sand of a color to match the rocks and use this to bind the structural units together into a unified whole.

For quickly gluing together objects with rough surfaces (rocks, corals, etc.) one can use Silastic silicone with great success.

Plastics

Nowadays it is incredible how many different things are made of plastic. There are several kinds of plastic which might have been specially created for aquarium work. There are plastic sheets varying in color and hardness, tubing of different calibers, some of which can be bent when cold, others when heated. There are hoses, rods and bars, nuts and bolts, hinges, transparent film and so on. Components made of the same plastic can easily be glued or welded together. Most plastics can also be glued

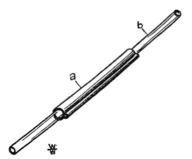

Tubing closure. a = tubing with flange along one side (extended), b = air-line, c = tubing closure bent.

to other materials. Whenever possible plastic should be used to replace metal objects that are constantly in contact with water. Colored plastic film of the appropriate tone is suitable for shading aquarium tanks that receive too much sunlight.

It is usually a thankless task to recommend materials, but I gladly do so in the case of plastics. In planning aquaria I often recommend PVC as the most suitable material. Whereas previously I only had at my disposal unsatisfactory substances such as glass or celluloid, I now reach almost mechanically for PVC and the problem is solved from the viewpoint of materials. It is immaterial whether the requirement is a system of tubing to go around six corners or a complicated aquarium tank. Nowadays air-lines are almost always made of plastic tubing. Here I may perhaps make a suggestion. The plastic tubing used in certain medical transfusion equipment is provided with a device for regulating flow which is simple in operation and ideal for our purpose. All other clips I have so far used are unsatisfactory in the long run. The device consists merely of a piece of soft plastic tubing ($1\frac{1}{2}$–2 inches long) with a firm flange along one side. The flange is thin enough to allow easy bending, but thick enough to hold the bent tubing in the required position and strong enough to withstand frequent bending without breaking. This regulating device is used when it is essential to deliver an exact number of drops per minute, and many aquarists are enthusiastic about it.

A number of styrofoam plastics have also been used in aquaria. Hard foam plastic is remarkably light, and it can be obtained in almost any thickness and also in large sheets. In decorating a tank the aquarist would often like to install large masses of rockwork but cannot do so because of the weight. In such cases foam plastic can be used to make excellent imitation rockwork. When touched with a hot object this material immediately melts and dents at the point of contact. So it is possible to model it into almost natural rockwork using a soldering iron. Crevices, caves and so on can be made in it, producing a truly three-dimensional effect. At first the shining whiteness of foam plastic is distracting, but after a week or two, when it has become covered with the first layer of brown algae, it takes on a more natural appearance.

In most of the soft foam plastics the enclosed air spaces are not in communication with each other. But there are foam plastics with a capillary-like structure, which are suitable for coarse mechanical filtration. They are easy to clean and can be re-used. Nevertheless, no foam plastic should be used until it has been tested and found to be non-toxic. Any of the foam plastics can, of course, be used as a shock-absorbing underlay for an aquarium tank.

Fine netting is made of nylon in various mesh sizes. These can be used for many aquarium purposes, for instance to separate different filter media in the filter or at the inlet to the filter to prevent small animals from reaching the filtration chamber. The same material is

Placing driftwood together with the mudskipper *Periophthalmus* is very appropriate. Mudskippers inhabit coastal waters and can get out of the water and crawl about on the tidal flats; they even can climb mangrove roots. Photo by Earl Kennedy.

used for cords and strings of various strengths, including fishing-lines. In fact, nylon cord can be used under water for a variety of purposes and it lasts for a long time.

Paints

As already mentioned, corrosible metals should be kept away from the aquarium. If it is impossible to avoid their use, then care should be taken to paint them properly. The experienced aquarist knows that over a period even the best quality paint has no chance against the persistence of water. A good solution to the problem is to coat the metal with epoxy resin.

Wood

Under the influence of humidity wood starts to warp and eventually decay, and wood glues, even the really good ones, lose their tenacity in the course of time, so here again wood components should be properly painted. Hardwood veneers are aesthetically satisfactory if properly fixed. On the other hand imitation veneers do not look right even if made of a material that is otherwise ideal for aquarium work. When a veneer becomes too damaged by humidity, it would be better to renounce the use of wood.

Timber and roots employed as decoration in an aquarium can, of course, be coated with polyester resin, if one wants to be quite safe. This will be unnecessary if such objects have been carefully chosen. Roots which have lain dead on the bottom of a river for several years will have rotted back to a core which is resistant to decay and thus relatively clean. This firm core or heartwood can be used in aquaria. Roots and timber dug up from peat moors are also quite safe in a tank, for they usually consist only of heartwood.

4.

The Decoration

Do it yourself—but do it properly

The task of decorating aquaria is not unlike the work of a garden architect, except that in the former the space and proportions are considerably reduced. The aquarist is faced with the unaccustomed task of creating a miniature yet truly natural landscape, which he has usually never in fact seen in the wild and only knows from verbal and pictorial description. He wishes to carry out the task properly so that his aquarium will be a real attraction to the observer. To do this it seems to me quite essential that he should first observe the original in nature. He should assiduously collect every scrap of information on the appearance of the underwater landscape which is to serve as his model. He must get a complete picture of such a landscape into his mind and have all the important details at his finger-tips.

Reduced to its basic essentials, any natural water contains a number of plants, rocks, sand, roots and so on. Taken together these constitute the aquarist's decorative material. He has to test and select, to arrange and position these until he has produced an aesthetically satisfy-

The arrangement of plants, rocks and other decorations in a tank is limited only by personal preference. However, certain fishes (like the angelfish, *Pterophyllum scalare*, shown here) require tall tanks and ample swimming space. Photo by K. Paysan.

ing whole. Naturally this is easier said than done. Surrounded by piles of decorative material it is always difficult to know where to begin. So I recommend that he should start in another way. First, put aside the decorative material for a while and try to look at the problem from the theoretical viewpoint.

The substrate normally consists of sand. If the sand used is all of the same grain size there will be little scope for variety, but even here there are two possibilities. The sand can be laid completely level or it can be arranged to form an attractive wavy substrate and the aquarist has then only to wait until the fish and the water movements have succeeded in levelling it out again. And that

The range of coral forms available for decoration is very wide, as shown in this photograph of a natural reef in the Maldives. Photo by Scheer.

they will certainly do! Completely level bottoms do occur in nature, but they do not look attractive in an aquarium, so it is better to construct a varied type of substrate in such a way that it remains in position. Nature shows us the best way of doing this. A mixture of fine sand and fist-sized stones, with all the intermediate sizes, will give a firm, wavy substrate which offers sufficient space and anchorage for plant roots. Here the larger stones, which support each other, form the framework of the bottom, while smaller stones in decreasing sizes, and sand, fill in the interstices and bind the whole together. To create this type of bottom requires plenty of time. The different sizes of stone, gravel and sand have to be collected and then the larger stones have to be carefully placed in position to give form to the whole. Flat stones are used for the hollows and dips, large round stones for the high places. At suitable spots, small pockets must be left and filled only with fine sand; these will later take groups of plants.

The informal impression made by everything beautiful in nature should not mislead us into thinking that the tank will be all the more attractive the more informal it is.

In planning an effective aquarium decoration there are two basic rules which are important for success. We must now concern ourselves rather more closely with these.

When using rocks, or any other material for decoration, the basic rule is: a main focal point to catch the eye and a counter-balance to provide contrast. These basic principles must guide all further considerations.

The main focal point of the group of three large elongated stones on the right is counterbalanced by the smaller, round stone on the left. The main focal point gives the impression of a typical array of rocks in an imaginary natural setting. The small contrasting stone emphasizes the accidental nature of the grouping.

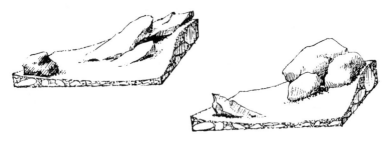

Elongated rocks with a round
contrasting stone.

Round rocks with an elongated
contrasting stone.

The same principle can be used but the roles reversed. Round stones form the main focal point, and the small flat stone provides the contrast.

Let us return once more to nature, where there are all gradations from the most beautiful panoramas to completely monotonous landscapes. Any aquarist who is not clear about the aesthetic function of one feature or another would be well advised to turn to the pictures of the great landscape artists to see the harmonious arrangement of pictorial elements. A knowledge of these will certainly ease the task of the aquarium decorator.

But to return to our experimental tank. We come now to a new element, namely roots and branches. Quite apart from their characteristic shapes, they can be used in the same way as the rocks. So a rather large piece of root can be set in the right background of the experimental tank, and here again a smaller, elongated root or branch enlivens the picture and provides contrast.

I would strongly recommend that anyone who wishes to decorate an aquarium should work from a model, at least in the beginning. For this an open box with floor, back wall and two side walls will suffice, and a length of 6 inches is enough. This is best made out of transparent material so that the results can be checked from all angles. On this small stage the decorative 'props', whether sand, rocks or roots, can be moved about at will until we are content with the result. The whole thing costs almost nothing and a great deal can be learnt from it.

Aquatic plants, which on biological grounds are the most important decorative element, present the most difficult task. Quite apart from the job of obtaining suitable species, they must first be balanced against one another according to size, and secondly they must be planted to allow for growth. An attempt should be made to have low-growing, turf-forming species alongside large, bushy plants. If possible the turf should be divided into a larger main patch and a smaller separate patch. All the components produce an informal whole. The proper use of sand and rocks, roots and plants has produced a decorated aquarium that is in accordance with the basic principles already established. Innumerable other decorative schemes can be carried out on the same principle.

The aquarist may see and admire a thicket of *Myriophyllum* in a lake and may try to reproduce it in his aquarium. He will soon learn to be critical and to correct his grouping if it looks too tidy and formal.

Diagram to show method of building up a firm substrate.

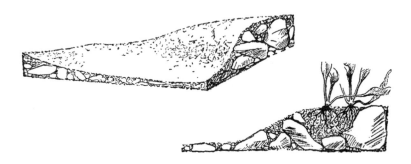

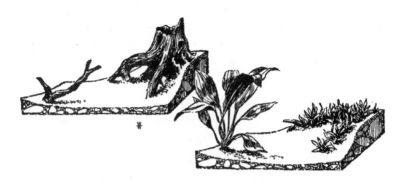

Root with smaller root as
contrast.

Turf of small plants with a
large plant as contrast.

The recollection of a stream bed with green underwater lawns may stimulate him to install a turf of, for
example, *Echinodorus intermedius.* A few grass-like
plants growing up behind stones or between roots also
improve the picture, which may be rounded off with a
particularly beautiful specimen of *Echinodorus panicu-
latus,* which dominates without destroying the whole.

If one looks at a piece of natural water and counts the
number of plant species, one nearly always finds that in
a restricted area there are relatively few species living
together. On large flat areas usually only one species is
dominant. So the vegetation in an aquarium tank should
also be restricted to a few species. Whether you believe
it or not, three species of plant, well suited to each other,
are considerably more attractive than a hodgepodge of
several different species, even if great pains have been
taken with the other parts of the decoration. Unfortunately the aquarium with several different species is still
fashionable among 'aquatic plantsmen.' I am certainly
not against having several plants, I am only against a
museum of plants.

There is yet another decorative element which must be allowed for. The free space in an aquarium is not only important for the fish, it is also very important visually. To avoid having an underwater jungle there should be a definite proportion of free space relative to the area taken up by fixed decorative material. As a rule the ratio of open to furnished space can be 50:50. But in some cases the ratio can be shifted to 70:30 in favor of the filled space.

An examination of the inner life of natural waters will soon yield a number of underwater landscapes which in their variety will provide a wealth of ideas. I am always astonished that so many aquaria are decorated as though by someone who had never looked at a stream, lake or pond.

A detailed examination of a river can be carried out along its length or across its breadth. At its source it may, for example, be a small mountain stream flowing in lively fashion over rocks towards the valley. Narrow enough for a child to leap over it, every few yards its

A combined waterscape.

Diagram of an undercut bank. a = asbestos plate, b = fastening for asbestos plate, c = roots.

bottom is filled up with stones, debris and old roots which have broken away from the banks. Usually there will only be vegetation along the banks or in the pools which occur here and there in places where the water flows more slowly. Delicate, fine-leaved plants seldom grow here and for miles there will be only one or two robust species. The stream bed will be dominated by rocks, sand and roots, to which a few tough algae and water-mosses succeed in attaching themselves.

The middle reaches of the river will be quite different. The flow is now more peaceful and bridges link the banks. Usually it is only possible to see the bottom near the banks, when the water surface is undisturbed and the sun is in a suitable position to give shadows and contrast. Here the banks are quite different, and the way in which they have been undercut, often up to a yard back, shows that they have long defied the water. The stones on the bottom have become smaller, and now and again on the inner sides of the bends there will be deposits of

Echinodorus plants are very popular because they are not only very hardy aquarium plants but also very diverse in form; examples are the large broad-leafed type above and dwarf grass-like form below. Photos by R. Zukal.

alluvial sand. In quiet corners protected from storms, and specially near the banks, there will be accumulations of humus and detritus, in which small thickets of plants will have started to grow.

The further we go down-river the muddier becomes the bottom and the richer the vegetation. In the lower reaches it is only the banks that are of interest to us, because only here is it possible to make observations. Even diving with a snorkel will scarcely allow this, because the water is now more or less cloudy owing to particles of suspended matter.

A glance at the different parts of a river in cross-section shows that the picture is essentially similar. There will be two banks, either steep or undercut, which slope away gradually to the center of the river bed. The shore zone provides the best model for aquarium decoration. One could use a section representing the upper, middle or lower reaches of the river.

Let us imagine a tank decorated to represent a small piece of flat, level stream bed and its banks. An imaginary bank is built on the back wall of the aquarium so that it gradually rises away from the viewer. Or we could take part of a cross-section through a stream as a model, making one side of the tank represent a bank. Alternatively, with a sufficiently long tank we could reproduce a complete cross-section, through the bed of a stream, making the two sides of the aquarium into the opposite banks of the stream.

A section through the middle reaches of a stream can be built up in the following way. One side of the aquarium represents the middle and deepest part of the stream bed, from which the bottom rises gently. The other side of the tank, that is, the bank side, is built up with stones and sand to give an ascending substrate, as already described. A pair of rocks placed on edge against the tank wall will give the impression of a shoreline. Above them one or two carefully selected roots can be fixed to the upper third of the side wall. The tips of the roots should reach out toward the center of the tank.

Plants can be put in where the roots allow the light to penetrate. This arrangement gives the impression of an undercut bank. The decorative roots are fixed to a sheet of asbestos or gray PVC that is exactly the same size as the side wall of the tank. If the roots are in several pieces they can be attached to each other by plastic screws or with nylon thread. They can be fastened in position by nylon thread running through holes in the side plate. This construction should be fixed firmly in position before the substrate is introduced. The rising bottom will hold the lower part of the side plate in position. The top of the plate can then be fixed by a couple of clamps to the upper edge of the tank.

If the tank is sufficiently deep and the shoreline has been built up on one side, the substrate can be so arranged as to give the impression of a slight bend in the bed of the stream. To do this the groove or channel representing the center of the stream bed can be made to run in a gentle curve toward the back of the tank. The plants can be arranged to strengthen the impression of a curve.

In an ordinary landscape, ponds and lakes provide the same kind of contrast as small islands in a large expanse of water. In addition to natural waters there are also numerous artificial ponds and lakes, and the older these are, the more closely does the configuration of their beds approach that of a natural lake. With a bottom of the same character, subject to the same range of environmental factors, it not surprising that both types should come to look alike after a number of years. In time, and depending on the nature of the bottom, a gradient towards the deepest parts is formed. If the

A large display aquarium reminiscent of a shallow stream bed close to the bank. Photo by Dr. D. Terver.

banks are not lined by sheer rocks or tree roots, a small step will appear, so that the bottom does not, in fact, run down quite evenly. Also, with a sandy beach there will often be a small step or ridge which marks the highest level reached by the water.

The characteristics of an underwater scene in standing waters can only be seen from the shore, but this does not really give a complete picture. So why not fit oneself up with flippers, mask and snorkel? Thus equipped the aquarist can explore every corner of a pond, provided the water is clear, and thus obtain a completely different, but more accurate picture.

Although most lakes show a certain uniformity, my diving trips have revealed that quite a number of places which looked attractive were typical of a pondscape and suitable for aquarium reconstruction.

Imagine, for example, that a small, underground stream runs into the shallow shore region of a pond. In the course of time it has made a shallow channel, perhaps 4–7 inches deep, in the falling bed of the pond. To reproduce this in an aquarium, we must first allow the substrate to rise towards the back of the tank. The small channel will look best if seen slightly from the side, so the substrate should be arranged to allow the channel to run diagonally from the back wall toward the glass. The bed of the channel should have relatively coarse pebbles grading at the edges to fine sand. This creates the impression that a stream of water has washed away the fine particles, leaving only those that are too heavy to be moved.

In nature, the sand at the inflow is very clean, in contrast to that in the surrounding areas. In the aquarium the opposite would probably happen very quickly, for all sorts of detritus would collect in the channel and the whole visual effect would be spoilt. So here a little trick must be employed: first, a root can be placed above the origin of the channel on the back wall, which will then lie in the shade; this also hides the back wall. In addition a few carefully placed plants will help. The next step is to install the outlet of the filter at the point on the back wall where the channel originates. The gentle stream of water from the filter outlet, which must of course be completely hidden, will then reproduce the natural conditions almost exactly. In nature, vegetation will start to grow at a certain distance from the channel, and this too can be copied in the aquarium.

At some time or other a pond I know has become enlarged, so that a tree which had for long grown on its banks came to be out in the middle of the water. I was able to recover the wood and since then have had an attractive root in shallow water. With most of it submerged and overgrown by water plants, this has now become an ideal hiding place for several fish. This

The inflow of an underwater stream.

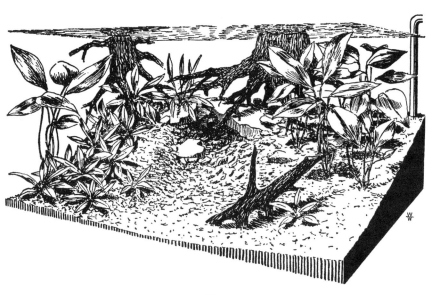

A large aquarium outfitted to suit the habits of a typical cichlid like *Hemichromis bimaculatus*. There are enough hiding places beneath the flat rocks and open sandy areas to satisfy their digging instincts. Photo by Dr. D. Terver.

underwater scene is particularly suitable as a pattern for aquarium decorations, in which for technical reasons the main point of interest has to be placed in the center.

Another quite typical pond scene is one in which a large root lies half buried in the bottom and at right angles to the gradient. A small cavity has formed underneath it, giving a marked step in the pond bottom. This can be very attractively adapted for an aquarium tank.

Technical know-how

Numerous technical snags will arise in the course of creating a new aquarium decoration. There may, for example, be a root which always floats up, or a piece of rockwork which is always falling down. Such things can be very annoying. But believe me, there is almost always a solution if one only thinks hard enough, or if one has sufficient experience. It is completely senseless to go to great lengths in shoring up a section of rockwork which will not stand up. The next time a fish has to be caught the whole thing can be guaranteed to fall down, and it may break a pane of glass. It is much more sensible to assemble the rocks properly and to fix them together with a good plastic glue, such as Silastic.

Roots which are continually being brought to the surface by buoyancy should be firmly fixed down once and for all. Stick a plastic nut firmly to a rock, using plastic glue. The root can then be bored and bolted to the rock. Plastic screws or bolts can also be used to stick two roots together. Small pieces can be simply tied together with nylon cord or thread. It is also not difficult to hollow out a whole tree trunk. This should be sawn or split into two halves longitudinally, and then carefully hollowed out with a large, semi-circular chisel. When dry, the two halves can be stuck together again.

The marine aquarist need not despair when his most beautiful pieces of decorative corals start to fall apart.

With silastics the damage can be quickly, permanently and cleanly repaired. Although they are expensive, these cements can be used very sparingly. Foam plastics, which are sometimes used in aquarium decoration, are exceedingly buoyant and can be firmly attached to the tank with these same silastics.

Kangaroos in a pine wood

I am sometimes astonished when I look at the usual kind of community tank. Nobody would dream of keeping an owl with a seagull, and decorating the cage with a palm tree. But this kind of thing is not unusual in aquaria, where one can see Angelfish from the Amazon alongside Asiatic Glass Catfish, or African characins in a tank with Platies from America. It is true that they are all bred fish which have never seen their native habitat, but they do, however, still retain their specific way of life and requirements. The vegetation, too, is all too often a hodgepodge of *Sagittaria* from America, *Cryptocoryne* from Ceylon and *Anubias* from Africa. Such confusion is very disturbing and will only please the observer who knows no better. But the aquarist should know better, and also he can do the job much better, because he has every opportunity. He also knows the requirements of the fish as regards food, light, oxygen and so on.

In some cases we do not know for certain whether certain factors are really important to the fish. For example, we suppose that they do not like living too close together (except shoaling fish). We also suppose that the behavior of their neighbors is of some significance, and that pleasant neighbors contribute greatly to their well-being. It is also accepted that a fish's environment, such as rocks, substrate and plants, has an influence on its behavior and health. Surely therefore we can avoid mistakes by giving the fish an environment that is as close as possible to that of their original habitat and by keeping them only with other fish which live in their home range. This leads us to an aquarium tank based on ecological principles. That is, not an all-purpose tank, but a reproduction of the underwater environment or biotope of a definite region. There are countless aquatic biotopes. Strictly speaking, every pond and every river is a different biotope. But to enter into such detail would be going too far. For the aquarist only a certain number of environments are of interest, for it is only from them that tropical fish are imported in any number.

It is not unusual to find life forms combined in a common tank like the one shown here with complete disregard of the geographical and ecological requirements of each species. The fishes and plants come from different areas of the world like Asia, North and South America and Australia and from diverse habitats ranging from open rivers to streams and swamps. Photo by W. A. Tomey.

For the sake of safety any rockwork installed in a tank should be secured by any of the methods recommended in the text. Unless attached firmly the coral piece on the right side of this tank set-up can topple down easily, possibly breaking the front glass panel. Photo by Dr. H. R. Axelrod.

This tank reflects the underwater conditions of Lake Malawi, Africa and is designed especially to house some well known members of the Mbuna like *Labeotropheus* and *Pseudotropheus.* Photo by Dr. H. R. Axelrod.

5.

Some Suggestions for Landscape Aquaria

Waters in the lowlands of S.E. Asia

With its great wealth of tropical fish, this habitat offers many possibilities. There are innumerable irrigation channels and canals, with stagnant offshoots, ponds and swamps, which form a paradise for labyrinth fish, species of *Rasbora* and *Aplocheilus* and so on. The banks are lined with reeds and bamboo thickets, and shaded by a wealth of tropical trees. The surfaces of such waters are usually so thickly covered with a tangle of floating plants that only a little diffuse light reaches the bottom. In the plains it is very hot from February to October when the average water temperature is about 28°C (82°F). From October to February it is somewhat cooler, and the water temperature drops to an average of about 23°C (73°F). The pH of these waters is low (about 5–6) and definitely acid. The hardness of the water fluctuates between 0 and 3 German degrees (DH). The substrate is usually dark and muddy. All this provides a quite specific picture and it is stimulating to use this as a pattern for an aquarium.

The most important feature of these waters is the wealth of floating plants. In the aquarium, therefore, there should be sufficient space (about 7 inches) between the surface of the water and the tank cover, with constantly moving fresh air. If the air becomes too humid the floating plants will be damaged, even though there

Decoration of an aquarium representing the lowland waters of S.E.
Asia. Fish illustrated (*from left to right*): 1. *Trichogaster leeri*,
2. *Betta splendens*, 3. *Rasbora heteromorpha*, 4. *Brachygobius
nunus*, 5. *Barbodes fasciatus*, 6. *Acanthophthalmus kuhlii*.

are no visible drops of condensation. A tilted cover
allows condensation water to run off. The roots of the
floating plants may become very dense and thus determine the character of at least the upper part of the tank.
The bottom looks best if slightly uneven. The sides and
rear of the tank can be decorated with shoots of bamboo
or reeds, each with one or two dried leaves left on; this
will do no damage and it looks more natural.

If the tank is large enough, one or two stout roots can
be fitted in, as though they belonged to a tree growing
on the bank. A small piece of root stuck in the sand provides the necessary contrast. For the substrate a fine
sand, as dark as possible, would be the most suitable;
in the course of time detritus will accumulate on top of
it and the resemblance to the natural model will be even
more striking.

Betta splendens, the Siamese fighting fish. Photo by R. Zukal.

Acanthophthalmus kuhlii, the coolie loach. Photo by A. Van den Nieuwenhuizen.

Trichogaster leeri, the pearl gourami. Photo by K. Paysan.

Rasbora heteromorpha, the harlequin fish. Photo by R. Zukal.

As already mentioned, it is typical of these waters that the ground vegetation is not very prolific. This is a feature which should be retained, and of course the dense covering of floating plants will restrict the growth of plants on the bottom. It would be best to have two or three species of robust plants capable of thriving in shade, as for example, *Aponogeton undulatus, Cryptocoryne grandis* and *C. nevillii* (the latter requires rather more light), or *Hygrophila*. The picture would be completed by the stems of a few water-lilies, such as *Nymphaea tetragona, N. pygmaea, N. alba minor* or of *Nymphoides peltata* and *N. indica*.

The water used should be at the correct temperature, hardness and pH, and care should be taken when pouring it into the tank. There should always be a few gaps in the covering of floating plants so that air-breathers, such as labyrinth fish, can take in air at the surface without difficulty. The usual floating plants used are *Eichhornia* (which requires plenty of space above water), *Pistia stratiotes, Lemna* (a tropical duckweed) and *Azolla pinnata*. The correct way to light such a tank is with fluorescent tubes, because the heat produced by ordinary tungsten lamps would damage the emersed parts of the plants. In tanks fitted with a circulation for filtration, there will be excellent air circulation from the pump's ventilation fan.

The tank, with its water and plants, should be kept about four weeks with normal lighting and aeration but without fish, so that the plants have a chance to take root. This will also give the aquarist plenty of time in which to decide on the make-up of his fish community. He will be able to consult the literature and scan the dealers' lists so that he eventually chooses a suitable selection of fish from the wealth of species originating in S.E. Asia.

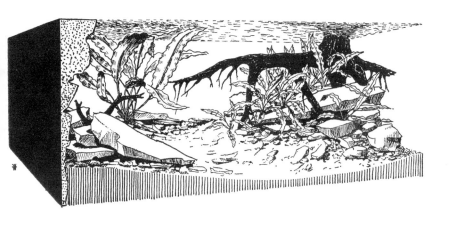

Decoration of an aquarium representing a mountain stream in S.E. Asia. Fish illustrated (*from left to right*): 1. *Labeo bicolor*, 2. *Botia macracantha*, 3. *Puntius nigrofasciatus*, 4. *Rasbora maculata*, 5. *Acanthopsis choirorhynchus*, 6. *Botia hymenophysa*.

Mountain streams of S.E. Asia

From the same general region come a number of interesting species which live, however, in clear, fast-flowing mountain streams. Some of these are very suitable for a landscape aquarium, as for instance the loaches which are typical inhabitants of this kind of habitat. These fast-moving streams force their way through gullies and erode the rocky soil. Their beds are therefore sandy and full of stones, which provide good hiding-places. Here, where the rain forests gradually rise up the mountains, bamboos and wild bananas shade the banks, and in places there are tree-ferns and giant trees entwined by lianas, on which beautiful orchids find their place in the sun. The water is rich in oxygen and well illuminated, because floating plants are completely lacking, and the

Botia hymenophysa, the banded loach. Photo by Dr. H. R. Axelrod.

Acanthopsis choirorhynchus, the long-nosed loach. Photo by R. Zukal.

84

Botia macracantha, the clown loach. Photo by H. Hansen.

Rasbora maculata, the pigmy rasbora. Photo by K. Paysan.

fish are lively and active. It is an environment which is attractive by reason of its lightness, cleanliness and liveliness.

Almost everywhere in this habitat the untiring, scouring water will have loosened little masses of rock. Angular pieces of rock, both large and small, fall into the stream, whose bed consists of round, polished pebbles. These provide the motif for a tank. Pebbles of various sizes can be collected from the nearest gravel-pit. They can be placed on the floor of the tank in such a way as to form an S-shaped ridge, thus suggesting a stream bed that has been irregularly eroded. One side of the tank has a carefully chosen piece of rock, sawn flat and positioned so it represents a rocky bank that is slightly overhanging. Smaller, elongated pieces of the same type of rock lie in groups on the pebbles, as though they had fallen from the banks; they provide good hiding-places.

The vegetation consists mainly of *Cryptocoryne* species, such as *C. undulata, C. griffithii, C. grandis* and *C. haerteliana*. But not more than two of these species should be used in any one tank, and they should be planted fairly densely and not too deeply. A well grown specimen plant of *Aponogeton crispus* will help to divide up the area of open water.

A root of suitable size protrudes from the right hand rear corner of the tank and is partly buried in the sand. This strengthens the impression of a fast, scouring stream. It is important that the different components of the picture should be present in the correct proportions. The sharp contrast between rock, sand and gravel on the one hand and a group of plants on the other gives the impression that a few plants manage to find a foothold even in such a frequently changing stream bed. It should again be stressed that this type of tank must have a number of hiding-places as these are essential for some of the fish species concerned.

In these waters the temperature normally fluctuates between 24 and 28°C (75–82°F), the pH lies between 5 and 6, and the water hardness is very low (0–3 German degrees). In choosing the fish for this kind of tank remember that, as for most aquaria, it is better to keep several fish of a single species than one or two of a number of different species.

In the present case, and depending on the size of the tank, one could have five or six *Labeo bicolor* (with only two specimens of this species there will be fights to the death), a large shoal of *Botia macracantha* and a smaller shoal of *Barbus nigrofasciatus* or *Rasbora elegans.*

Puntius nigrofasciatus, the black ruby barb. Photo by M. Kocar.

Labeo bicolor, the red-tailed black shark. Photo by Dr. H. R. Axelrod.

Rasbora elegans, the two-spot or elegant rasbora. Photo by Dr. H. R. Axelrod.

Barbodes lateristriga, the T-barb. Photo by Dr. H. R. Axelrod.

Puntius conchonius, the rosy barb. Photo by R. Zukal.

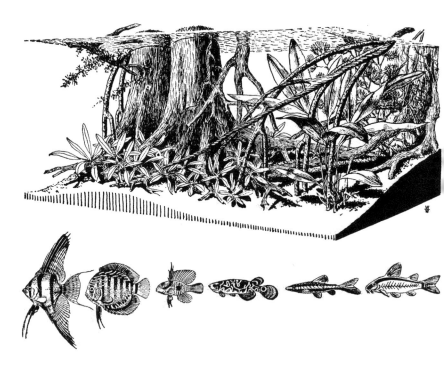

Decoration of an aquarium representing the waters of the Amazon region. Fish illustrated (*from left to right*): 1. *Pterophyllum scalare*, 2. *Symphysodon discus*, 3. *Apistogramma ramirezi*, 4. *Rivulus ocellatus*, 5. *Poecilobrycon eques*, 6. *Corydoras arcuatus*.

Rain-forest waters of South America

It has been said that the Amazon region, which with its endless profusion of rivers, lakes and swamps almost bisects a whole continent, produces more decorative fish than any other part of the world. But this is not the only reason for choosing a section from this rain-forest river as model for a landscape aquarium, nor is it because this is the habitat of the Angelfish. One of the special attractions of this vast area is its changeability; the waters are enormously swollen during the rainy season but become shrunken during the dry period of the year. For this reason the rivers do not have firm banks but are surrounded by areas that are subject to flooding. Along the edges there are tangles of roots, tree trunks and branches that have been washed down from the upper reaches of the river.

In this great area there are three different river types which can be distinguished by the form of their beds and particularly by their water. The main part of the river, with its so-called 'white water', carries muddy cloudy water, and so it is not of interest to the aquarist. Our aquarium fish come from the other two river types—the clear water and the 'black' water. The clear water streams come from a region in which immense rainstorms keep the bottom scoured, so that there is scarcely any suspended matter. This water is clear and clean.

Corydoras arcuatus, the skunk catfish. Photo by G. J. M. Timmerman.

Symphysodon aequifasciata, the discus fish. Photo by M. Kocar.

Cabomba is a popular plant kept by aquarists. Photo by S. Frank.

In places the clear water gives way to 'black' water, which is colored brown by humic substances which have dissolved out of trees and other plants. Such water is still clear. The water temperature fluctuates between 25 and 30°C (77-86°F) and the pH between 4.5 and 6.5. The water is almost comparable to distilled water, having a hardness that is nearly always less than 1 degree German (DH).

During the greater part of the year the shoreline trees and bushes in the rain-forest stand about three feet deep in water, so that their roots are scoured. The aerial roots of epiphytes thrust their way in among the stilt roots of the trees, and branches and tree trunks rot away in the water. Odd pieces of timber float gently at the surface, overgrown with grasses and epiphytes. In places where the sunlight reaches the water there may be carpets of floating plants. Above all this towers the age-old rain-forest, which is being continually renewed. Secretive, yet bewildering in its manifold beauty, but cruel to everything that is too weak to hold its own, it will be no surprise that this is the habitat of many predatory fresh-water fish. An Amazon aquarium should be somewhat shadowy and bizarre, rather than merely pretty.

Here the back wall of the tank can be covered with a sheet of asbestos, to which roots and curved branches can be attached. At the rear and to the left, two roots are fixed to the sheet in such a way that their lower ends are about 2-4 inches above the substrate. Their stems extend above the water surface, to give the impression of trees standing in the water. One of the two trunks has been split vertically, so that the part retained, say two-thirds of it, can be fixed flush to the back plate. The other stem has only had its roots trimmed to allow them to interlace with those of the first. The tropical stilt roots can be imitated by using the slightly curved and branched roots of an alder, which is a not uncommon tree on the banks of ponds and streams. The illusion of a rain-forest can be increased by fixing a stem of wild honeysuckle to imitate a liana hanging in the water. If space allows, a *Philodendron* can be grown in a pot alongside the tank, so that its aerial roots hang down into the water. The substrate can be of rounded black pebbles of basalt which will give a close approximation to the bottom of a rain-forest stream. It would be best, however, not to reproduce the layer of dead leaves and humus which is characteristic of such a stream. A dense patch of several *Echinodorus tenellus* or *E. intermedius* planted under some of the tree roots extends to about the center of the tank. At the back on the right, where there are only a few roots, there are some plants of *Cabomba aquatica* or —for beginners—*Myriophyllum brasiliense.*

A picture taken during the dry season of a stream showing the characteristic roots of the trees extending into the water. Photo courtesy of the American Museum of Natural History.

Poecilobrycon eques, a pencilfish. Photo by R. Zukal.

Apistogramma ramerizi, the ram, or Ramirez's dwarf cichlid. Photo by H. J. Richter.

Apistogramma agassizi, Agassiz's dwarf cichlid. Photo by R. Zukal

A small "black water" tributary of the upper Amazon in Brazil. Photo by Dr. H. R. Axelrod.

The information given in the literature on the occurrence of the different fish species in the Amazon region is very inconsistent and inexact. This is probably due in part to the fact that the various species are not really restricted to a given biotope. So it is not always possible to say whether they require 'black water.' The decoration suggested is typical of the region with such water. Since a large number of the available decorative fish occur in 'black water', it would be quite in order to use such water in the tank described. Aquarist dealers now offer some good preparations with which one can prepare 'black water.' Experiences with peat filters for producing acid water are so contradictory that I really cannot recommend them for this purpose. The water should certainly be slightly acid, but it must be well buffered.

Cheirodon axelrodi, the cardinal tetra. Photo by R. Zukal.

Copeina arnoldi, the jumping characin. Photo by R. Zukal.

The fish will usually also tolerate a water that is kept at around neutral pH; such water is also more stable.

Out of the large number of fish available from this region I will only make a few suggestions. The tank might for example be stocked with three to five *Pterophyllum scalare*, a few *Corydoras aeneus* and *C. melanistius* or *C. punctatus julii* (the same number of each), two to three *Callichthys*, *Carnegiella strigata* and *Hemigrammus pulcher*. The selection might be completed with a somewhat larger number of *Paracheirodon innesi* or *Cheirodon axelrodi* and a pair of *Copeina arnoldi*. Another possibility would be to stock the tank with some *Symphysodon*, a pair each of *Apistogramma agassizi* and *A. ramirezi*, a larger number of *Rivulus urophthalmus* and a few *Aequidens maronii* and *A. curviceps*.

Carnegiella strigata, the marble hatchetfish. Photo by H. Schultz.

Pterophyllum scalare, the angelfish (black marble variety shown here). Photo by H. Smith.

Aequidens curviceps, Thayer's cichlid. Photo by Kremser.

Cichlasoma festivum, the flag cichlid. Photo by R. Zukal.

The waters of an African rain-forest

In Africa there are several underwater habitats that should be of great interest to the aquarist. There are rain-forest pools and slow-flowing streams with dense vegetation, all supporting large populations of fish. As a result of various expeditions, many of these are now regularly on the market. It is no wonder that they are regarded as ideal aquarium fish, for they hold their own in a jungle of vegetation, in stagnant, muddy, oxygen-deficient water, teeming with large numbers of competitors. So they have all the attributes necessary for a long life in the aquarium.

Pantodon buchholzi, the butterflyfish. Photo courtesy of the New York Zoological Society.

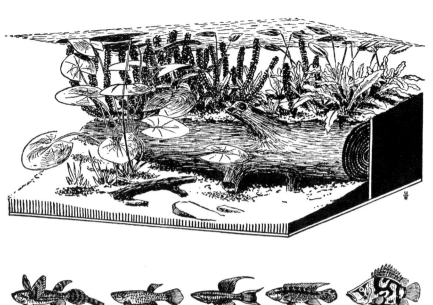

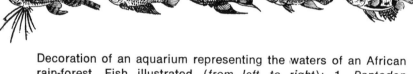

Decoration of an aquarium representing the waters of an African rain-forest. Fish illustrated (*from left to right*): 1. *Pantodon buchholzi*, 2. *Epiplatys macrostigma*, 3. *Aphyosemion bivittatum*, 4. *Pelvicachromis taeniatus*, 5. *Polycentropsis abbreviata*.

To design an attractive tank with a thicket of aquatic plants is not so easy as it might seem. On the one hand we want plenty of plants, but on the other we require sufficient free space. The problem can, however, be solved very elegantly by making an unusually high step at the rear of the tank, using a tree root cut down the middle so that it looks like a piece of wood that has fallen into the water. To do this, make a bottom plate of asbestos and at right angles to it glue on a strip of asbestos of the appropriate height; this strip can be supported behind by a couple of struts. The tree root is placed so as to hide the bottom plate and the vertical strip. In this way one can form a step 7-10 inches high

Epiplatys sexfasciatus, the six-banded panchax. Photo by H. Hansen.

Epiplatys macrostigma, the spotted panchax. Photo by H. Hansen.

Aphyosemion bivittatum, the lyretail. Photo by Col. J. J. Scheel.

Aphyosemion australe, the Cape Lopez lyretail. Photo by Col. J. J. Scheel.

Neolebias ansorgei, Ansorge's neolebias. Photo by G. J. M. Timmerman.

and divide the tank in such a way that the lower level occupies about a third of the bottom area of the tank. Both levels rise gently towards the back and give the impression of a shallow shoreline interrupted by a treetrunk. On the right, beneath the trunk, there is a cave, as though scoured clean by the water. Here again the substrate can be of dark basalt, with a few rocks and pieces of root arranged naturally. On the upper level towards the left there is a thicket of *Lagarosiphon muscoides,* which becomes less dense towards the center. On the same level, but to the right, there is a similar but rather smaller group of *Aponogeton distachyus.* On the lower level, to the left, there is a single specimen plant of *Nymphaea baumi.* If possible, it would be pleasant to cover a part of the water surface with a species of *Trapa*. The water should be slightly acid and kept at 25-30°C (77-86°F).

In this region one of the most interesting genera is *Ctenopoma*. These are labyrinth fishes, and some of the species could be used in the kind of tank I have just described. Two or three Butterfly Fish (*Pantodon buch-holzi*) would live well at the surface among the floating plants. The remaining inhabitants can be chosen from among the wealth of fish available from this part of the world provided they are generally peaceful.

Aphyosemion cognatum, red-spotted aphyosemion. Photo by G. Senfft.

Phenacogrammus interruptus, the Congo tetra. Photo by Dr. H. R. Axelrod.

Aplocheilichthys katangae, the Katanga lampeye. Photo by Dr. H. R. Axelrod.

Pelvicachromis pulcher, the kribensis. Photo by Kremser.

Aphyosemion sjoestedti, the blue gularis. Photo by Col. J. J. Scheel.

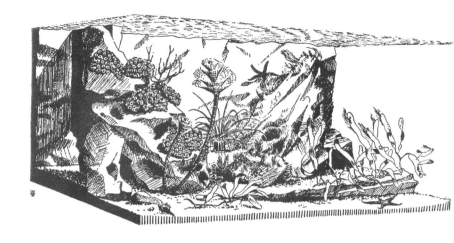

Decoration of a Mediterranean aquarium. Fish illustrated (*from left to right*): 1. *Serranus scriba*, 2. *Dentex vulgaris*, 3. *Coris julis*, 4. *Blennius ocellaris*, 5. *Crenilabrus scina*.

Temperate marine aquaria

In northern temperate regions, sand and rocks are the most important decorative elements for a marine aquarium. At first sight these may appear somewhat inadequate, but in recent years self-contained diving and underwater photography have shown how diversified a sea bottom of sand and rock can be.

The fauna of the sea is very rich in species and the struggle for existence is constant and fierce. It is therefore important to select the correct species. The normal population of a temperate marine aquarium, representing for example the North Sea or Mediterranean, would consist of sea anemones, starfishes and sea urchins, sea-cucumbers, hermit crabs and other crabs, tube-worms, snails, a few bottom-living fish and also occasionally some free-swimming fish. This type of aquarium can be attractively decorated without a great deal of trouble, and at the same time made to suit the requirements of several animal species.

The fine white sand sold for aquaria is very suitable for this purpose. It resembles white sea sand but does not become so compact and always remains permeable. Sea-shells and pieces of coral, the souvenirs of past holidays, can be ground down in a mortar and mixed in with the sand. The junk box becomes emptier but the aquarium substrate assumes a more natural appearance.

Most marine animals require shelter and hiding-places, so the decorative rockwork should have holes and crevices. Dolomite is, therefore, very suitable for this purpose, because its rather bizarre appearance closely resembles that of a shore where the rocks have been tunnelled by innumerable generations of marine boring animals. As a model for a marine tank, let us take a place on the sea bottom where a cliff face rises from a bed of sand on which lie a few pieces of rock.

Stone masons will often be able to supply a suitable piece of rock for the background. This should be smooth on one side where it is fitted against the rear glass, and rough on the front face. On the right, in the rear, a piece of longish pointed rock is placed in such a way as to represent a cliff salient. If necessary, it can be shored up at the base. Do not be concerned about using more than one kind of rock, because in quite a short time they will all become coated with algae and present a completely uniform appearance. To the left, in the front third, a small cave has been constructed out of several pieces of rock stuck together with epoxy glue. To the rear of this, a single flat stone placed vertically and reaching to the

Coris julis, a Mediterranean wrasse. Photo by Kremser.

Blennius pavo, the peacock blenny. Photo by H. Hansen.

Serranus cabrilla, the comber. Photo by K. Paysan.

Serranus scriba, the banded perch. Photo by K. Paysan.

rear wall of the tank encloses a chamber to house and hide an internal filter, which will still be easily removable. A hole should be left leading from the bottom of the cave into this chamber. The space between the cave on the left and the diagonally placed stone on the right is spanned by a further piece of rock and the area behind it is filled with sand, rising gradually towards the background rockwork. To prevent this sand from trickling down through cracks and crevices we can resort to a trick gleaned from observation in the sea. There I have often found groups of empty bivalve shells which the waves have jammed into the spaces between the rocks, packing them so closely as to form a barrier. The same can be made artificially in the aquarium, but here it would be best to stick the shells together with Silastic. This works well and looks very natural. In the right foreground a longish piece of rock forms a small ledge with a space behind it which can be filled with sand that falls gradually towards the flat bottom immediately in front of the left-hand cave. Whenever possible it is a good idea to grow a little *Caulerpa prolifera*. This is a marine alga which does well provided it has sufficient light and a chance to become attached—so at the start no fish or sea urchins should be put into the tank. When conditions are right a small piece of this alga will grow into a handsome clump. The whole effect will be agreeably enhanced by one or two small pieces of gorgonian. It is also a good idea to add a handful of empty gastropod shells to provide new and larger 'houses' for any hermit crabs which may later be put into the tank. This kind of set-up can be used for keeping invertebrates or fish or both. There is a wide choice of animals, and in every case it would be best to learn everything possible about them before making a final choice. A table giving all the possibilities would be far beyond the scope of the present volume.

A barrier of bivalve shells.

Tropical marine aquaria

I have an idea that it is easier to decorate a marine tank properly than it is to describe the actual operation. The more bizarre the natural model is, the quicker are we attracted, because we have no scale by which to judge it. Nobody could say that a coral reef is monotonous, but the continuous repetition of the bizarre can be monotonous. This can easily happen in an aquarium if the job of decoration is not done very critically. The first impression of a coral tank is striking on account of its strangeness, but over a period of time its decoration can appear very uniform, particularly if only dead white calcareous structures are used.

On a coral reef the individual coral colonies usually sit with their bases on a compacted mass of dead or dying coral branches, which are permeated and glued together by innumerable calcium-secreting organisms. So there is a striking contrast between the loosely branching corals above and the massive foundation below, and this offers the aquarist a good opportunity to create something richly varied.

Let us first take stock of the position. We have at our disposal coral stocks or branches with a base, sand, pure

Amphiprion frenatus, the red clownfish. Photo by K. Paysan.

Pomacanthus semicirculatus, the Koran angelfish. Photo by H. Hansen.

rock, possibly a large decorative bivalve (e.g. *Tridacna*) and the free water space. It is very regrettable that the coral stocks offered for sale usually have no base at all. Apparently the collectors break them off clean at the base. Indeed, one has the impression that they carefully avoid leaving even the tiniest piece of base attached to the coral. If they did so it would greatly enhance the value of the coral to the aquarist. One could always break it off if it was inconvenient. So, in fact, all that can be done is to improvise and reconstruct a base as

Chaetodon auriga, the filament butterflyfish. Photo by Yasuda and Hiyama.

Due to the difficulty of keeping invertebrates in an aquarium it is not always possible to provide anemonefishes with the sea anemones in which they live in their natural environment. Photo by G. Budich.

Decoration of a coral-fish tank. Fish illustrated (*from left to right*):
1. *Pomacanthus semicirculatus*, 2. *Chaetodon auriga*, 3. *Zanclus
cornutus*. 4. *Pterois volitans*, 5. *Rhinecanthus aculeatus*, 6. *Amphiprion percula*.

neatly as possible. This can be done by sticking small
snail shells, bivalves or pieces of broken-up coral to a
base of dolomite, using Silastic cement. A diluted white
polyester glue can be run into the cracks and crevices,
and this gives a very natural effect. The coral stocks can
then be glued on to the block. The whole structure
should look as though it had developed naturally, but
of course there is the difficulty of cleaning such an
unmanageable object. Here the aquarist must himself
decide between an attractive appearance and practical
manipulation.

A large marine tank with several species of fish from tropical areas of the Pacific and Atlantic. Photo by Dr. D. Terver.

Chaetodon trifasciatus, the redfin butterflyfish. Photo by Dr. W. Klausewitz.

In one example, the left foreground of the bottom is covered with sand which rises gradually to a rocky ledge. In the background, and running from right to left, is the main thicket of coral firmly attached to its base, which has various holes and crevices. In places the coral branches rise to half the height of the tank, and some of them overhang towards the front. In the left foreground there is a single coral standing on its own base, giving 'contrast' to the whole composition. A giant clam shell (*Tridacna*) can be half-embedded in the sand; it should not be too large, but in proportion to the aquarium as a whole. As already described, the sand is mixed with broken shells and strewn with small pieces of coral. If a few sprigs of a tropical species of *Caulerpa* can be obtained, these should be planted in the sand and not in among the corals. The tank should then be kept without fish until the algae have had a chance to become attached. In spite of this the aquarist must become resigned to the fact that eventually some of the fish will simply annex his beautiful patch of algae. It would be bold to suggest which coral reef fishes should be kept, in view of the great variety of these attractive marine creatures. It is, however, essential to learn about the habits of the fish before buying them. The selection of suitable species will itself give you the greatest pleasure.

Pterois volitans, the lionfish or turkeyfish. Photo by G. Marcuse.

Rhinecanthus aculeatus, the Hawaiian triggerfish. Photo by Karl Probst.

Zanclus cornutus, the Moorish idol. Photo by Dr. J. E. Randall.

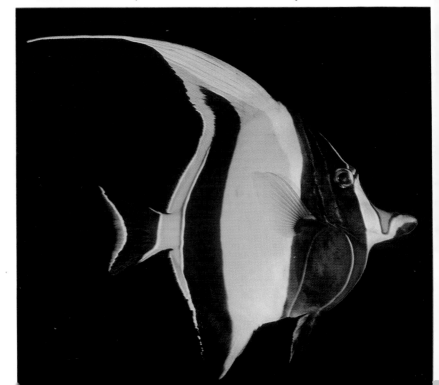

Tridacna, the giant clam. Photo by Dr. H. R. Axelrod.

Index

A

Acanthopsis choirorynchus 83, 84
Acanthophthalmus kuhlii 79, 80
Aequidens curviceps 99, 101
Aequidens maronii 99
Aeration 7
Africa tanks 102-103, 106-107
All-glass tank 19
Amazon 97
Amazon tank 90
Amphiprion frenatus 116
Amphiprion percula 119
Anemone fish 118
Anubias 75
Aphyosemion australe 105
A. bivittatum 103, 105
A. cognatum 107
A. sjoestedti 109
Apistogramma agassizi 97, 99
Apistogramma ramerizi 90, 96, 99
Aplocheilus 78
Aplocheilus katangae 108
Aponogeton crispus 86
A. distachyus 106
A. undulatus 82
Artificial fertilizer 12
Azolla pinnata 82

B

Barbodes fasciatus 79
Barbodes lateristriga 89
Betta splendens 79, 80
Black water 94, 97

Blennius ocellaris 110
Blennius pavo 112
Botia hymenophysa 63, 84
Botia macracantha 83, 85, 87
Brachygobius nunus 79

C

Cabomba aquatica 95
Callichthys 99
Carnegiella strigata 99, 100
Caulerpa 122
Caulerpa prolifera 114
Cement 16-18, 48
Chaetodon auriga 117, 119
Chaetodon trifasciatus 122
Cheirodon axelrodi 98
Cichlasoma festivum 101
Copeina arnoldi 99
Coralfish tanks 115, 119, 120
Corals 58, 79, 119, 122
Coris julis 110, 112
Crenilabrus scina 110
Corydoras aeneus 99
C. arcuatus 90, 91
C. melanistius 99
C. punctatus julii 99
Cryptocoryne 75, 86
C. grandis 82, 86

D

Daphnia 9
Decoration 56
Dentex vulgaris 110
Dermogenys pusillus 10

E

Echinodorus 65
E. intermedius 95
E. tenellus 95
Epiplatys macrostigma 103, 104
Epiplatys sexfasciatus 104

F

Filter media 6
Filters 23, 24, 25, 29
Floating plants 78-79, 82
Food 9-10

G

Glass 46
Glues 51

H

Hardness 87, 94
Hemichromis bimaculatus 72
Hemigrammus pulcher 99
Hiding places 71, 111
Hygrophilla 82
Hyphessobrycon flammeus 11

L

Labeo bicolor 83, 87, 88
Labeotropheus 77
Lagarosiphon muscoides 106
Lakes 67, 70
Lemna 82
Lighting 16-17, 23, 24, 26, 36

M

Marine aquaria 110-111, 114-115,
   118-119, 122-123
Mountain streams 83
Myriophyllum 61
Myriophyllum brasiliense 95

N

Neolebias ansorgei 106
Nitrate content 8
Nymphaea alba minor 82
N. baumi 106
N. pygmea 82
N. tetragona 82
Nymphoides indica 82
Nymphoides peltata 82

P

Paints 55
Paludarium 31, 33-35
Pantodon buchholzi 102, 103, 107
Paracheirodon innesi 99
Pelmatochromis thomasi 49
Pelvicachromis pulcher 109
Pelvicachromis taeniatus 103
Periophthalmus 54
pH 78, 87, 94
Phenacogrammus interruptus 108
Philodendron 95
Pistia stratiotes 82
Plastics 52-54
Poecilobrycon eques 90, 96
Polycentropsis abbreviata 103
Pomacanthus semicirculatus 116,
   119
Pseudotropheus 77
Pseudotropheus auratus 47
Pterois volitans 119, 123
Pterophyllum scalare 57, 100
Pumps 7
Puntius conchonius 89
Puntius nigrofasciatus 83, 87
PVC 41, 52, 67

R

Rasbora 78
Rasbora elegans 87, 88

R. heteromorpha 79, 81
R. maculata 83, 85
Rhinecanthus aculeatus 119, 124
Rivers 64, 66
Rivulus ocellatus 90
Rivulus urophthalmus
Rockwork 48-49
Roots 54, 55, 60, 62, 64, 67, 70, 71, 74, 79, 95

S

Sagittaria 75
Sealers 48
Serranus cabrilla 113
Serranus scriba 110, 113
South America tanks 90, 94-95, 98-99
South Asia tanks 78-79, 82-83, 86-87
Stainless steel tank 18

Symphysodon aequifasciatus 92
Symphysodon discus 90

T

Tank base 25, 30, 37
Tank size 39
Trapa 106
Trichogaster leeri 79, 81
Tridacna 117, 125
Triturus vulgaris 34
Tubifex 9
Tubing 52

W

Water plant 11, 12
White water 91,
Wood 55

Z

Zanclus cornutus 124